# PRESENT TRENDS
# IN CHRISTIAN
# THOUGHT

*By L. Harold DeWolf*

AN ASSOCIATION PRESS
**REFLECTION
BOOK**

ASSOCIATION PRESS · NEW YORK

PRESENT TRENDS IN CHRISTIAN THOUGHT

———

*Copyright © 1960 by*
*National Board of Young Men's Christian Associations*

———

Association Press, 291 Broadway, New York 7, N. Y.

Grateful appreciation is herewith expressed to the National Methodist Student Movement for its permission to use in this book some of the materials formerly appearing in *Trends and Frontiers of Religious Thought*.

50 cents

*Library of Congress catalog card number: 60-6569*
Printed in the United States of America

*Gratefully dedicated to all my students and readers who have talked back and so assisted with my education.*

# CONTENTS

# CHAPTER ONE

# THE NEW SURGE OF RELIGIOUS THOUGHT

Religion would soon disappear among civilized people. This prediction was freely made from the middle to the end of the nineteenth century and later.

"God is dead," announced Nietzsche's Zarathustra.

"Religion is the opium of the masses," declared Karl Marx. He assured his readers that all belief in God would disappear when the Communist revolution had done away with the suffering of the poor under capitalist exploitation.

Belief in God was only the rationalization of hidden emotional drives, explained Sigmund Freud. As for Christianity, one could now write its epitaph under the title, *The Future of an Illusion.*[1]

All such death notices of religion proved premature, to say the least. Even in the Soviet Union,

* Footnotes will be found at the end of each chapter.

where Marx's revolution took place two generations ago, Christian faith is very much alive. Through all these years the Communist government has pushed the most intensive scientific education, the most materialistic philosophy, and the most clever anti-religious propaganda in all history. Religion not only has survived, but has undergone a vigorous rejuvenation since World War II. Thousands of Christian churches are regularly crowded with worshipers, and countless multitudes of people maintain Christian faith and life in informal and underground associations.

In the United States the churches face such a large increase in church membership, attendance, Sunday school enrollment, giving, and recruitment for the ministry that it seems too good to be true. Is all this new popularity of religion a mere fad without depth of conviction or even of concern?

Though on the fringes of the Christian movement there are doubtless many easy conformists and many evidences of shallow self-deception, at the center there are deep currents flowing. There are people who, in the name of Christ, are challenging the most deeply entrenched injustice, at the cost of reputation and at the risk of life. There are countless others who engage in tireless labors of faith and love, caring for the sick, poor, and imprisoned, without pay, instructing and counseling youth, battling for clean government, and devoting long hours to the prayer from which they draw their strength.

One of the most important features of the present scene is the quantity and quality of hard religious thinking which appears in print. There has not been such intense and searching study of the Christian faith in the centuries since the Protestant Reformation. Actively participating in this intellectual and spiritual inquiry and discussion are representatives of such distantly separated bodies as the Eastern Orthodox and Baptist, Lutheran and Methodist, Anglican and Quaker, Roman Catholic and Congregational churches.

This book will introduce the reader to some main types of recent religious thinking by Christian theologians. It is impossible to represent the full richness and power of any important theology in so brief a treatment, but it is hoped that this little volume will serve as a guidebook. Perhaps like other guidebooks it can extend the horizons even of readers who go no further. It is hoped that it will also draw many to high adventure in reading from various authors here represented and help such travelers to find their way to the most valuable treasures.

The author is an American and a Protestant. American thought bulks larger in this study than it would in a similar survey by a European, and this book deals chiefly with Protestant theology. However, a number of Europeans and some Roman Catholic and Eastern Orthodox writers are considered.

One characteristic of recent religious discussion is the breaking down of familiar distinctions between traditional and even relatively modern schools of thought. Most writers have read so widely and learned so much since World War I from thinkers of traditions other than their own that classification has become uncommonly difficult. You cannot know in advance along what lines a Quaker and a Greek Orthodox lay theologian will differ. Recently in a public meeting a distinguished Unitarian scholar was heard seriously protesting to an Episcopalian that the latter had missed the truth in the doctrine of the Trinity! Even the lines dividing such more recent movements as Fundamentalism and Modernism, Neo-Orthodoxy and Existentialism, have been crossed and recrossed by so much intellectual traffic that they have become blurred.

Despite the problems and objections, it is possible and desirable to classify the recent trends of thought in a general way. Such classification will be useful so long as its significance is not misunderstood.

It must not be supposed that because two thinkers are named as representatives of the same trend they will be found usually in agreement. Sharp differences occur within every one of the trends delineated. On the other hand, highly important agreements link together various trends. In an evening of discussion on a particular problem the lines of division will often cut directly across such classes as are depicted in this volume.

The reader who finds himself choosing a given trend or school of thought and then feels bound to defend it thereafter, regardless of cost to integrity or evidence of truth will be in a most unenviable position. It is hard enough to be obedient to God and loyal to truth without being bound at the same time to this or that school of thought. Most of the thinkers with whom we shall have to do are too much in earnest to be much concerned about any such conformity. Classifying them may therefore seem arbitrary.

Nevertheless, there *are*, in current Christian thought, *trends which differ notably and even radically*. A northeast wind and a northwest wind are thoroughly different in direction and effects, even though in some respects they are similar and even though a meteorologist cannot draw on a map lines which precisely mark their boundaries, even for a day. So each of the trends described in the following chapters differs in important respects from every other, and the debates between their representatives are fraught with momentous consequences.

After describing each of the various trends, the author acknowledges certain positive values contributed by its representatives to the Christian churches. Then he lists some objections. The stating of objections does not mean that he dismisses every trend as false, any more than he accepts every one as true because he finds value in it. Any reader who thinks that his favored views are treated too roughly should at least observe that the author has stated grave objections to the trend which he himself represents, along with the others. In every instance, effort has been made to report some of the more plausible and serious criticisms urged by representatives of various rival views. In no case has the author sought to pass a final judgment. He has sought only to guide the reader into earnest, critical thought on major issues. No view should be dismissed merely because some serious objections have been raised against it, until a better doctrine has been found. What view is best the reader is invited to decide for himself. No one can take from him that privilege and that solemn responsibility.

## NOTES

1. London: Hogarth Press, 1928.

# CHAPTER TWO

# LIBERAL THEOLOGY

Christian thinkers must define in every age the relations between their faith and the contemporary culture. Since culture is always changing, the task is never finished. In periods of rapid development the need for it becomes especially imperative. We live in an age of unparalleled breadth, depth, and speed of change in science, economics, politics, and modes of living. Hence the task of recent theology has been both extraordinarily urgent and also more complex than ever before.

There are two basic ways by which Christian thought and life may respond to secular culture. There are also more complex modifications of these, some of which are helpfully discussed by H. Richard Niebuhr in his book *Christ and Culture*.[1] One basic and direct response is by accommodation to culture. The other is reaction against it. In the present chapter we are considering some theologies of accommodation to our secular culture. The first aspect of the present culture which appeared to threaten faith was science. It was primarily in accommodation to the empirical sciences that liberal theology was begun.

## MODERATE LIBERALISM

Among the theologians who would, in various ways and degrees, modify the traditional interpretations of the Christian faith in adaptation to our science-dominated culture, we observe first the moderate liberals. They regard themselves as unequivocally Christian, maintaining the essential affirmations of Christian doctrine. They think these affirmations to be sound and true. Because they are true they may, without fear or favor, be subjected to all the tests and evidences which reason can muster. The moderate liberals believe that truth will have the best chance to win over error in the open arena of honest, critical examination. They believe also that doctrines ought to be stated as clearly and intelligibly as possible, in forms which make evident their relevance to contemporary life.

These moderate liberals have high respect for scientific method; they do not agree with all the ideas which are recommended in the name of science. For example, though accepting biological evolution, they reject the view that man is "only another animal." Though encouraging and participating in psychological inquiry, they vigorously deny that man's conduct is rigorously determined by causal law, to the exclusion of free and responsible choice. At the same time, they grant the propriety of critically examining also religious ideas, wherever found, in the open-minded search for truth. They make use of philosophical methods in their inquiries, and often move easily between philosophy and theology.

They accept wholeheartedly the use of textual and historical criticism in the study of the Bible, while taking the Bible seriously as a great storehouse of divinely inspired wisdom. Some parts of the Bible they regard as much more valuable and authoritative than others. Supremely important are the accounts of Jesus and his teachings.

The human nature of Jesus is stressed, but he is also believed to be uniquely endowed and uniquely faithful as revelation of God in human history. Jesus' death is regarded as the climactic seal of his faithful life. The moderate liberals generally reject the idea that Jesus' death fulfilled requirements of God's justice. This, they think, would make Jesus superior in character to God or set up an intolerable contradiction between God's love and his justice. The implied notion of retributive justice is a conception long taken for granted in human law but now inacceptable even in that context, let alone ascribing it to God himself. The crucifixion of Jesus reconciles men to God only as it changes their attitudes and character.

Generally, these thinkers emphasize strongly the need to apply Christian principles, not only to personal life, but also to the solution of the great social problems of our time. The theological stress on such application, from a liberal point of view, is often called "the social gospel." This name is given especially to the teaching of several American Protestants, all born in the nineteenth century, such as Walter Rauschenbusch, Washington Gladden, and Francis J. McConnell. Such present moderate liberals as John C. Bennett, Walter G. Muelder, and Martin Luther King, Jr.,[2] continue this emphasis, but in changed historical and theological context. All these men, both the earlier and present ones, have felt deeply the desperate sinfulness of man. They have seen that much of this sin is imbedded and perpetuated in social relations and institutions. Believing that the power and love of God can outmatch all other powers, they have sought to give appropriate and healing expression to this faith in social policy. They have been especially concerned with the selfishness and materialism presupposed and fostered by much current economic policy, the sensual indulgence of conspicuous consumption, the denial of brotherhood between races and classes, and the warring hostilities of the nations which threaten world catastrophe.

Moderate liberal theology was given systematic expression near the beginning of this century by William Newton Clarke and William Adams Brown.

In the nineteen thirties, Albert C. Knudson used a method of historical analysis and the philosophical arguments of a critical post-Kantian personalism for the construction of his system. In 1953 was published my own systematic theology in a volume entitled *A Theology of the Living Church*.[3] Walter M. Horton, whose *Christian Theology: An Ecumenical Approach*[4] is finding wide use, describes me, along with himself, as "neo-liberal." By this description he means to indicate that we have learned much from recent neo-orthodox writers, though opposing some of their most characteristic emphases and continuing to use basically liberal methods. I would acknowledge the truth of this description. I differ from my theological teacher, Albert C. Knudson, in deriving theology more directly from the testimony of the Bible, and in taking sin more seriously as a spiritual condition and a humanly inescapable social involvement. Unlike Knudson, I avoid making my theology dependent on a particular philosophical system.

John Baillie, devout, liberal Scottish Calvinist, has influenced both American and British thought, with important forays into theological debates on the Continent. In *The Idea of Revelation in Recent Thought*[5] he vigorously refutes the doctrine of "plenary" (that is, complete) inspiration of the Bible, and yet he acknowledges the supreme authority of the revelation reported in the Bible by fallible, though inspired writers. *The Belief in Progress*[6] is one of the best comparisons of the modern ultimate hope in earthly progress with the New Testament hope. The latter, he holds, includes the hope for significant and large achievement on earth, but looks also beyond this insecure environment. In one of his earlier books, *And the Life Everlasting*,[7] he argued persuasively that without God, everlasting life would be undesirable as well as improbable, but that if we believe in God then we should both desire and expect to live forever by his free gift— that is, by divine grace.

His equally gifted brother, Donald M. Baillie, was later in coming to recognition and also earlier in departing from this earthly scene. Christendom will long be indebted to him for his study of the Person of Jesus, entitled, *God Was in Christ*.[8] So persuasive and so deeply rooted in Scripture and history was it that his book has evoked favorable notice from thinkers of widely diverse viewpoints. His stress on mystery and certain insoluble paradoxes might lead some to consider him an adherent of neo-Reformation theology. However, the systematic rational argument of his work, and especially his explanation of the Incarnation by analogy with man's experience of freedom and dependence on divine grace are points of affinity with the evangelically minded liberals.

Robert L. Calhoun is especially well-known for his solid historical grounding of theology and for his challenging book *God and the Common Life*.[9]

His liberal spirit and method are there made clear as he subjects historic Protestant doctrines to sympathetic, but discriminating, rational criticism, using criteria of theoretical and practical coherence.

Nels F. S. Ferré is an especially hard man to classify. Seeking to mediate between the moderate neo-Reformation theology of the Swedish Lundensians and the rational, open-minded philosophical method which he came to appreciate in studies under Edgar S. Brightman and Alfred North Whitehead, Ferré has so far succeeded as to place himself near the neo-Reformation boundary of liberal theology.

The most famous liberal Christian in the pulpit is surely Harry Emerson Fosdick. In his younger days he was the target of especially determined attacks by conservative Christians. Even at the age of eighty he was still wielding a thought-provoking and influential pen. The one world-renowned woman theological scholar is also a liberal of evangelical spirit. That is Georgia Harkness, who has written several little books of devotion and others for lay instruction, but also the fine scholarly work, *John Calvin: The Man and His Ethics*,[10] and the much later concise volume, *Christian Ethics*.[11]

Norman Pittenger is an Episcopal high churchman who calls himself a Catholic modernist. He combines high churchly views of the church and its ministry with liberal methods, an irenic, reasonable spirit, and many liberal interpretations of ancient dogmas.

The late Archbishop William Temple not only had much to do with launching the ecumenical activities which have merged in the World Council of Churches; he also exercised much theological influence of his own. Though loyally and sometimes exclusively Anglican, Temple exercised generally a moderating and reasonable influence in theology. His Gifford Lectures, *Nature, Man, and God*,[12] set forth confirming evidences of wide variety to support some of the main doctrines which we have learned from church and Bible. He held that the task of natural (rational or philosophical) theology was not to construct a true system of thought about God and human destiny, but rather to criticize and confirm revealed theology and to serve as a channel of communication with unbelievers.

J. V. Langmead Casserley has contributed both to the Church of England and the Protestant Episcopal Church in America several brilliantly written books the spirit and method of which are well symbolized by the title of the most important one, *Graceful Reason*.[13] He persuasively defends natural theology against recent theological detractors, while stressing our utter dependence on God's grace.

Several philosophers have been notably helpful in encouraging the co-operation of philosophy and theology in the ways recommended by moderate liberals. Among such philosophical writers must be mentioned Julius S. Bixler, who is further from traditional Christian positions than are most of the theologians named, and Edgar S. Brightman, personal idealist and devout churchman. In Great Britain, W. R. Sorley is known for his elaboration of a moral argument for God, and F. R. Tennant's "wider teleological argument" has probably influenced recent British and American philosophical theism more than any other approach.[14] William Ernest Hocking, versatile idealist, continues to write brilliantly even after years of retirement from teaching. Peter A. Bertocci, influenced chiefly by Brightman and Tennant, is author of *Introduction to the Philosophy of Religion*,[15] widely used in college classes.

George F. Thomas stands squarely on the boundary between philosophy and Christian theology, clearly distinguishing them, but seeking to relate them coherently. Especially influential is his *Christian Ethics and Moral Philosophy*.[16]

Moderate liberalism in all its forms, has had to stand against certain powerful social forces of the day. We live in a time of revolutionary changes in our whole way of life, a time of extreme mobility, and of threatened total nuclear warfare. Hence there is a widely prevalent air of insecurity and even desperation.

Moderate liberalism is essentially a mediating position. Such a position is always especially hard to maintain in a time of crisis and revolution. Tense emotions, frayed nerves and desperate fears seek radical, colorful, extreme solutions. An interesting situation now presents itself. The effort to state the Christian faith in terms accommodated to modern culture has brought the moderate liberal theologians into opposition to both the prevailing mood and much prevailing practice of our culture. Accommodating Christian teaching considerably to scientific and rational methods for determining truth, they find themselves opposed ever more strongly to popular irrational moods and to political and economic policies which are anything but reasonable or Christian.

Faced with this situation some liberal preachers, habituated to a mood of accommodation, have fallen into easy acquiescence in the social evils of the day. Taking their cue from a popularized and perverted psychology they soothe their distraught congregations with comforting palliatives, pointing easy and conventional ways to peace of mind. No theologian of importance lends support to such perversion of the gospel, but the pulpit dispensers of reassurance have their reward from other quarters.

## NATURALISTIC THEOLOGY

Some more radical interpreters of Christian doctrine have moved toward a forthright alliance with naturalistic philosophy. This alliance distinguishes them from such liberals as we have been discussing, who are allied rather with various theistic, usually ideal-istic, philosophies. The naturalistic theologians tend to doubt or deny a personal life after death and to question the belief that God is a conscious, pur-posive Being, that is, personal. There are wide differences among these men, and some oppose vigorously the positions of others. Nevertheless, they do show in common the tendency to accommodate to naturalistic thought.

Vergilius Ferm is a well-known liberal Lutheran scholar. He is irenic in spirit and in his wide dis-cussions appears at times to approach the kind of viewpoint which we have characterized as moderate liberalism. Ferm has rendered invaluable service as editor of several volumes in which many theologians of diverse perspectives have collaborated, including the convenient and indispensable *Encyclopedia of Religion*.[17]

Daniel Day Williams may belong among the moderate liberals. He is devoutly concerned with the great Christian affirmations and is conciliatory in spirit. Yet his philosophical sympathies appear to be naturalistic. He presented one of the earlier and more penetrating critiques of the New Reforma-tion theology, especially its tendency to pessimistic and negative appraisal of man.[18] He has contributed also a widely read survey of contemporary theology, entitled *What Present-Day Theologians Are Think-ing*.[19]

Henry Nelson Wieman belongs at the more radical side of the group, near the boundary between a Christian orientation and an outright naturalistic humanism. However, he identifies himself with the Christian movement, uses much traditional Christian language, and has exerted important influence on Christian theology in America. Indeed, a number of strong Christian leaders who now maintain theological positions much nearer the center of the Christian tradition confess their indebtedness to Wieman for having given them important intellectual and spiritual help at a critical period in their lives.

Wieman shows clearly the influence of John Dewey's instrumentalism and of Alfred North Whitehead's process philosophy. He stresses the need to make theology thoroughly empirical and seeks therefore to say concerning God only what experience supports. God, for Wieman, is "the source of human good."[20] There is such a source, for much that we value is actually present. The source is partially identified with human society, for much of our good is a social heritage. Yet even human society is made possible by conditions in our universe which existed before any man and which produced men with all their values. On the other hand, both society and the nonhuman forces of our world not only create and sustain good. They also threaten, restrict, and destroy good and threaten to destroy all human life. By definition, God is the sum of the forces creative of good. More characteristically, however, Wieman thinks of God in relation to all the specific moments when good is created. God is the Creative Event. A man is a created event. The power and meaning of the Creative Event are seen especially clearly in the career of Jesus Christ.

Wieman shuns any developed system of ideas concerning the nature of God. The affirmation of concepts not supported by our experience leads to indefensible speculation. Besides, what is most needed is not the elaboration of concepts, but rather the coming into such relation to the Creative Event as will release in and through us His creative resources. If we set up systems of ideas about God we may then find ourselves shut up within these ideas of ours, instead of being open to God's ever new creative power.

Probably this passion for reality, the determination to know and represent God as he is experienced, without the stultifying of thought and life by presupposed intellectual structures, has, more than anything else, given to Wieman his greatest constructive influence.

However, Wieman's thought is a much more inspiring starting point than resting point in theology. Many have been helped by him, but few, if any of these, have continued to hold his theological position.

In the effort to avoid confining God within the

intellectual structures of traditional theological affirmation about God, Wieman seems to some of his students to have actually set up more confining structures by negation. He is so eager to avoid making traditional affirmations about God that he is even led into an apparent self-contradiction in the effort to escape them.

The supremely religious act of a man, according to Wieman, is prayer; for in prayer we seek to become channels of the Creative Event. Experience in prayer shows that its most creative heights are scaled when God is thought of as personal. Wieman thinks we ought not to believe that God is truly personal, since personality is experientially associated with a biological organism, but in order to close the circuit of a creative relationship we need, at the time of prayer, to think of Him as personal. Wieman believes that this need is due to the fact that we are persons and hence, in our weakness, need to think of God as a person. It is a symbolical supposition, not literally true, but useful.

If Wieman is right, then at the very moments when we are at our highest level of relationship with the Creative Event, in order to sustain this relationship we must entertain an idea which we have intellectually dismissed. Is this a position to be commended to every earnest and honest man? Is this rather the point at which experience itself supports a more generous affirmation of faith?

## VALUES OF LIBERAL THEOLOGY

We may well ask, at this point, what appear to be the greatest values contributed by liberal theology, and, more generally, in theological accommodation to a scientific culture. In making these statements we cannot do justice to any particular liberal. The concrete, living whole of every theologian's thought is far more complex and rich in meaning than any general classification in which he can be placed. Moreover, we are not attempting here to give final judgments concerning any type of theology, but only to introduce the reader to the current theological argument.

1. One purpose which has motivated much writing and preaching by liberal Christians has been to put the Christian message in terms understandable and persuasive to the people of the present age. Even in the New Testament, such books as Paul's Letter to the Romans, the Gospel of John, and the Letter to the Hebrews adapt the form of the Christian testimony to different groups and cultures. So Justin Martyr and others in the second and third centuries reformulated Christian teaching for appeal to people trained in Greek philosophy. Without some such active commerce of ideas with the surrounding culture, could the Christian religion keep relevant and effective?

2. Liberal theology insists upon open-mindedness to new evidence from all quarters. If the genuine

Christian message is true, as Christians believe it to be, the faith would appear to have much to gain by such an attitude. The very adoption of this spirit shows confidence in the truth of what Christians have to say. By their own open-mindedness they invite all who have dogmatically rejected the Christian faith to join in re-examination of its claims. To enclose the gospel in a protective wall, with "No Trespassing" signs posted against the sciences and other "secular" interests, would be to isolate faith from much of life and doom it to a sequestered irrelevance. When theology is in meaningful interaction with other contemporary thought, opportunity is afforded to Christianize all thought and life.

3. Critical literary and historical methods have been eagerly used by liberal theologians in the interpretation of the Bible. Seeking to assign a date to the fashioning of Eve from the rib of Adam or to Jonah's fabulous submarine voyage would seem to most present theologians like trying to locate Thomas More's Utopia on a map. On the other hand, unless we wish to assign Isaiah's prophesying, St. Paul's missionary journeys, and the life of Jesus to similar unearthly realms we cannot reasonably escape the task of discriminating historical study. In practice, the historical study of the Bible has illuminated many passages with rich new meaning and provided new grounds of confidence in the events most significant to the intelligent Christian.

4. It is largely under liberal leadership that the churches of America have renewed a concern with the social implications of the Christian faith. Rediscovery of the radical social implications of Christianity was, in no small measure, due to historical criticism in biblical study. The characteristic stress of liberals on ethics and on the teachings of Jesus has strongly reinforced this influence. A gospel which is addressed to the individual in abstraction from the social institutions in which a large part of his life is lived and by which all his life is deeply affected, is addressed to only half a man and is only half a gospel. The leadership in social concern provided by liberal Christianity in America is no small contribution.

## OBJECTIONS TO THE LIBERAL MOVEMENT

Some theologians are unimpressed by such claims for liberal theology. Others would gladly grant them and yet would raise serious objections to the liberal movement. Some churchmen who continue the liberal tradition would still think it needful to correct certain weaknesses of the movement.

1. One unfortunate effect of liberal theology, it is said, has been to discourage and reduce the use of the Bible by laymen and even by parish ministers. The denial that every printed page of the Bible had the absolute authority of God caused many people to conclude that the Bible had no

authority and was not worth reading. Moreover, reading with understanding was now said to be a much more demanding task than had been supposed by many glib quoters of proof texts. Biblical study in historical perspective seemed a highly technical task, better left to a few professional scholars. Since the liberals were also teaching that much of religious truth could be learned from contemporary literature and observation, one might as well let the Bible go, and turn to more understandable sources. It is hard to see how a vital Christian church can be long maintained without both ministers and congregations drawing deeply on the great sources of our faith. Many liberal theologians have taught and exemplified serious Bible study. Nevertheless, one effect of the liberal movement has been to reduce the use of the Bible by persons not biblical specialists.

2. A second liability of the liberal movement is its predisposition to gradualism. Partly through its mood of accommodation to culture and partly through the influence of secular evolutionism, liberals have tended to expect advances in both personal and social life solely through slow processes of education and growth. This preference for gradualism was partly offset by the wave of optimism which supported the hope to win "the world for Christ in this generation." However, after the blight of World War I, the trend to evolutionary thought became more dominant. In place of calls to repent-

ance, conversion, and dramatic change, the tendency of later liberalism was to place confidence in the slow processes of education and small increments of reform. Gradual progress is undoubtedly one way in which nature, history, and individual life move. But revolutionary and decisive moments of transcendent importance also occur, and such possibilities are ignored at our peril. To neglect their importance is to have only a partial view of life and to neglect the urgency of certain unequivocal decisions which we are called upon to make.

3. A third critical question about liberal theology concerns a certain tendency to substitute this-worldly trust in human achievement for a world-transcending confidence in God. Whatever may be the accomplishments of human effort, such an ethic if divorced from ultimate trust in God and from hope reaching beyond the bounds of this earthly life would bear little resemblance to historic Christianity. Would such an ethic be adequate to provide poise and strength to meet victoriously the perils of the present age?

The last critical questions suggest others. Are there other respects in which liberals have so far accommodated the Christian message to modern secular culture as to betray its priceless truth and its saving power in individuals and society? Some critics would raise questions about liberal teachings on the person of Christ, the meaning of the cross, justification by faith, the meaning and practice of prayer, and other important elements of historic Christianity. Few Christians would doubt that in the naturalistic extremes the Christian faith has nearly lost its identity.

Where, then, should accommodation stop? This is a crucial issue which confronts everyone who sets foot on the path of liberal theology. This question and the critique of liberal theology will be explored further in the succeeding chapters. All the other theological movements to be examined include much implicit and explicit criticism of liberal theology, as well as displaying much indebtedness to it.

## NOTES

1. New York: Harper & Brothers, 1951.
2. That Martin Luther King, Jr., is an able religious thinker, as well as man of action, will be evident to anyone who reads his *Stride Toward Freedom* and also his doctoral dissertation, *The Conception of God in the Theologies of Paul Tillich and Henry Nelson Wieman* (Boston: Boston University Ph.D. dissertation, 1955).
3. New York: Harper & Brothers, 1953. Cf. my more recent book, *The Case for Theology in Liberal Perspective* (Philadelphia: Westminster Press, 1959).
4. New York: Harper & Brothers, 1955, 1958.
5. New York: Columbia University Press, 1956.
6. New York: Charles Scribner's Sons, 1951.
7. New York: Charles Scribner's Sons, 1951.
8. New York: Charles Scribner's Sons, 1948.
9. New York: Charles Scribner's Sons, 1935.
10. New York: Henry Holt & Company, Inc., 1931.
11. New York: Abingdon Press, 1957.

12. London: The Macmillan Company, 1934, 1949.
13. Greenwich, Conn.: Seabury Press, 1954.
14. See Tennant, *Philosophical Theology* (Cambridge, Eng.: University Press, 1928-1930), Vol. 2.
15. New York: Prentice-Hall, Inc., 1951.
16. New York: Charles Scribner's Sons, 1955.
17. New York: Philosophical Library, 1945.
18. See his book *God's Grace and Man's Hope* (New York: Harper & Brothers, 1949).
19. New York: Harper & Brothers, 1952.
20. Cf. his book, *The Source of Human Good* (Chicago: University of Chicago Press, 1946).

# CHAPTER THREE

# FUNDAMENTALISM AND EVANGELICALISM

"Fundamentalism" is an effort to reaffirm the fundamentals of the Christian faith, in vigorous reaction and protest against liberal theology. The name is taken from a series of twelve booklets entitled *The Fundamentals*[1] of which about three million copies were distributed throughout the English-speaking world by two wealthy laymen, Milton and Lyman Stewart. The series constituted a popular defense of conservative Protestantism.[2]

Liberal accommodations to modern culture seem to fundamentalists to be betrayals of the Christian gospel. Such betrayals must be met, they believe, by a return to the Bible and the faith of our fathers. Yet, in common with every theological movement in history, fundamentalism shows clearly special marks of its own time and place. Its concern with liberalism tends to provoke particularly heavy stress on those doctrines, methods and attitudes most threatened by liberal theologians and by the scientific culture to which the latter have accommodated.

## FUNDAMENTALIST EMPHASES

1. Among liberals, especially of the more radical types, there is often a vague ambiguity of doctrinal statements, sometimes with the use of symbolic language which does not mean, in the usage of the liberal, what the words mean to the traditional Christian or to the uninitiated. Against all such vagueness and equivocation the fundamentalists place crisply stated, definite creeds. Although making some provision for figurative language, they are alarmed by liberal abuses of figurative interpretation and tend to lean over backward in *literal* affirmation of ideas which appear in Scripture, hymns, and ritual. They leave little room for uncertainty or reservation before problems regarded by many Christians of many opinions, present and past, as mysteries in which we can see only dimly. They tend to classify religious ideas in sharp, bold relief, as true or false, good or bad.

2. Against the predominantly philosophical method of some liberals the fundamentalist asserts a doctrine of biblical infallibility. Presupposing the truth of this doctrine, which has often been affirmed or implied in classical Christian writings and in the creeds of the churches, he endeavors to prove his

positions by the quotation of proof-texts. If every statement in the Bible is true, then all you need to prove a point is one good scriptural quotation which clearly affirms that position.

3. Against the use of historical criticism in Bible study, the fundamentalists charge that men are putting their historical surmises against the inspired word of God. The divine revelation is often simply identified with the text of the Bible now in use, usually the King James Version, regarded as miraculously given and preserved without error. Even textual criticism, based on recent discoveries of ancient manuscripts and fragments, is generally viewed with suspicion or open hostility. More recently, an increasing number of fundamentalists have been studying New Testament Greek. Some have accepted, among English translations, the Revised Standard Version of 1952, while others have made the most unrestrained attacks upon it. In general, fundamentalists oppose significant revisions of the biblical text and any interpretations out of harmony with familiar, popular understanding of the King James Version.

4. Against the accommodation of liberalism to a science-dominated culture, many fundamentalists, especially in the twenties, responded with a denunciation of the culture itself. Pointing to the religious skepticism of some prominent scientists and philosophers, they stirred popular suspicion of higher education into active hostility. Many young people

have been exhorted by fundamentalist preachers against endangering their souls by going to college.

Although some conservatives continue such attacks on education, most fundamentalists now employ a different strategy. Concentrating their attacks on "worldly" or "godless" schools, they urge their young people to attend "safe" or "good Christian" colleges, usually Bible schools under fundamentalist auspices.

5. Against the doctrine of evolution was hurled an angry denial. Evolution, said the fundamentalists, was a wicked and mistaken guess of pseudo-scientists, denying the sacred teaching of Genesis and implying that men were the children of apes, rather than of God. Evolutionary theory was attacked, not only because it was degrading to man and contrary to Scripture, but also because it seemed contrary to the traditional Christian doctrine of the Fall. If the evolutionists were right, said the fundamentalists, then man was not fallen from a state of original righteousness, but rather risen from the brutes.[3]

6. Opposing the liberal faith in the dignity and moral power of man, the fundamentalists have laid heavy emphasis on the Fall. Many assert the total depravity of man. Some reject total depravity, yet stress depravity. All would agree that human beings are spiritually helpless without a miraculous infusion of the divine grace.

7. The liberals tend to emphasize the humanity

of Jesus and to represent Christ as the model and symbol of what all men ought to become, but the fundamentalists typically put a one-sided emphasis on the deity of Christ. The ancient Church Fathers were concerned with defending belief in the humanity, as well as the divinity, of Jesus. Formally, the fundamentalists, too, would say that Jesus was both man and God. But because it was his divinity that was in question among the liberals, the fundamentalists have stressed the divinity, or rather "deity" of Christ to such an extent as to bring neglect, and even occasional implied denial, of his humanity.

8. In this stress upon the deity of Christ the fundamentalists often stress the Virgin Birth in ways without parallel in Christian history. The Virgin Birth has been traditionally affirmed by orthodox Christians as God's *sign* or *witness* to Christ's divinity, but not as the *meaning* of that divinity. The fundamentalists, on the other hand, often say that to deny the Virgin Birth is to deny the deity of Christ and make him only another man.

Moreover, they often assume that to call Jesus the son of God is to affirm that God was his father just as Mary was his mother. Such aberrations are the work of men lacking proper education in church history and trapped by their own emphasis on plain talk easily understood by the untrained mind. More sophisticated conservatives, even those identifying themselves with fundamentalism, are, of course, embarrased by such crudities.[4]

9. Modern culture is not congenial soil for belief in such miracles as seem to involve the violation of well-established causal law. Hence liberal theology, in its historical criticism, discounts many of the miracle stories in the Bible as only parables or as evidences of legend making by prescientific tradition. Fundamentalism, in its mood of defiance toward all such cultural accommodation, lays special stress on the miracle stories and depends heavily on them as proofs that the wonder-workers were fulfilling God's plans or possessed divine authority.

10. In contrast to the liberal stress on social applications of Christian ethics, fundamentalists interpret the gospel almost or altogether exclusively in terms of individual salvation. When confronted with war, political corruption, race discrimination, or economic injustice, they cite biblical prophecies of evil times to come. Sometimes, when they regard the social evils as curable, they say that if you can convert enough men to Christ, then Christian solutions of social problems will be quickly reached, because social institutions will be controlled by Christian individuals. In general, the fundamentalist response to all social problems is simply further preaching of the gospel of individual salvation.

1. infallibility of Scripture
2. virgin Birth
3. reality of miracles (Jated efforts)    5. Second Coming
4. Resurrection

## THE NEW EVANGELICALISM

As most fundamentalists have moved from a general hostility to culture and education toward a more discriminating position, they have developed an increasing number of well-educated thinkers. Some of these men have found it necessary, in the light of their more searching biblical and historical studies, to modify certain fundamentalist attitudes and teachings.

The men who are involved in this later development among religious conservatives are many. In some respects one would need to include the evangelist Billy Graham. His eagerness to co-operate with ministers and churches of varying theological points of view, his stress on the basic moral requirements of the Christian gospel, and his growing interest in social problems, like race relations and international peace, mark him as a man of broader and more humane outlook than that of the typical early fundamentalist leaders. At the same time, his constant introduction of proof-texts with the indiscriminate words, "The Bible says," his stress on individual conversions by techniques of the mass revival, and his literal acceptance of all the miracle stories, identify him with the fundamentalist movement.

More sophisticated and deliberate efforts at theological revision have been made by such men as Cornelius Van Til, Edward John Carnell, Carl F.

H. Henry, the veteran fundamentalist leader Samuel Craig, and the pastor of Park Street Church in Boston, Harold Ockenga.

At the inauguration of Carnell as president of Fuller Theological Seminary, Ockenga published, in a special bulletin of the Seminary, a significant article entitled "Theological Education." Note especially the following passage:

For decades fundamentalism has proved itself impotent to change the theological and ecclesiastical scene. Its lack of influence has relegated it to the peripheral and subsidiary movements of Protestantism. Wherever fundamentalism and modernism came into test in theological struggle, fundamentalism lost every major battle in the historical field. It has demonstrated little power to crack the social situation challenging the church today. The motivating loyalty to fundamentalism on the part of many Christians lies in its orthodoxy, its faithfulness to the Word of God. However, the judgment of history on fundamentalism is that it has failed.

The new evangelicalism embraces the full orthodoxy of fundamentalism but manifests a social consciousness and responsibility which was strangely absent from fundamentalism. The new evangelicalism concerns itself not only with personal salvation, doctrinal truth and an eternal point of reference, but also with the problems of race, of war, of class struggle, of liquor control, of juvenile delinquency, of immorality, and of national imperialism. It even faces the question of creeping socialism, and asks, is it Christian? The new evangelicalism believes that orthodox Christians cannot abdicate their responsibility in the social scene.

What are the principal revisions of fundamentalist theology to appear in the literature of this new evangelicalism?

1. There is a noticeable, though indecisive change in the doctrine of biblical inspiration and authority. Some of the new evangelicals, unlike most of the fundamentalists, avoid teaching "verbal" inspiration of the Bible, stressing rather plenary or full inspiration. This marks a movement to a more flexible position. A good example is in the scholarly work of the influential Nazarene theologian, H. Orton Wiley.[5]

Van Til and Carnell have further modified fundamentalist teaching by reviving and restating an old idea which formally preserves the doctrine of biblical infallibility but insulates it against the more obvious objections. They teach that because of mistakes in copying and translating, our present Bible is not infallible in detail, but the Bible as first inspired by God was perfectly free from error. The *autographa*, or original manuscripts of the biblical books, were infallible, because miraculously inspired. God has miraculously guided the transmission of the text in such a way that in matters necessary to our salvation, our Bible is still infallible. We may therefore use it as religiously authoritative, in an absolute sense, while we have at hand a ready explanation for such objections as the discrepancies among manuscripts, the contradictions between different passages concerning certain dates, and other details of peripheral interest.[6]

2. These scholars are ready to agree with liberal theologians that biblical texts ought to be studied in literary context. Some would go further and agree that whatever we can learn about the times in which a given passage was written may be of value. This means, despite disclaimers, that at some points the conservative is brought into study and discussion of the historical or higher criticism of the Scriptures. He is likely to return to condemnation of such an approach whenever he sees it threatening the traditional interpretation of a passage. Yet it is significant that a historical approach has been begun. The new evangelicals are in the forefront of the conservatives who approve and, indeed, urge study of the Bible in the original Hebrew and Greek.[7] Some of them, like Carnell,[8] give high praise to the careful criticism which has brought us ever nearer to authentic ancient texts.

3. In regard to the sciences in general, and particularly in relation to the biological theory of evolution, some concessions are being made. The conflict between science and Scripture is played down, and some adaptations in interpretation of both are introduced to minimize or eliminate contradictions. Sometimes it is granted that the evolutionist has correctly described the order in which

the various forms of life appeared on the earth—an order in general conformity to the order presented in the first chapter of Genesis. At the same time it is emphatically denied that the higher forms of life, especially man, evolved out of earlier and lower forms. Rather, each species (or vaguely defined kind) was a special new creation, even though it might differ but slightly from the last earlier species.

4. We have already observed Harold Ockenga's criticism of fundamentalism for its lack of concern with social problems. An earlier and much longer publication on the same subject was Carl Henry's book, *The Uneasy Conscience of Modern Fundamentalism*.[9] Another evidence of rising social concern is the appearance at Fuller Theological Seminary of the periodical *Christianity Today*. It must be added, however, that there is little in that journal which would disturb even the most conservative defenders of wealth and special privilege.

This new social concern is actually a cautious renewal of an interest which was a consuming passion in the revivalism of the midnineteenth century. Anyone who supposes that there is an inherent and necessary connection between conservative Protestant theology and the social conservatism or indifference which has recently characterized it should read Timothy L. Smith, *Revivalism and Social Reform in Mid-Nineteenth-Century America*.[10] The present *Christianity Today* looks very mild, indeed, as compared with many evangelical publications of that earlier period.

5. Even the stress on sharply defined, exclusive doctrine shows signs of softening. A trend toward greater flexibility has developed, largely under the influence of efforts to bring together conservative Calvinists and Arminians, Baptists and Nazarenes, Lutherans and Free Methodists. This requires considerable breadth of dogmatic tolerance. Observe, for example, a book by Samuel Craig, long recognized as an authoritative fundamentalist spokesman. In *Christianity Properly So-Called*,[11] he speaks explicitly of many doctrines which, he concedes, may be disbelieved by genuine Christians, even though Craig himself thinks they are true. Some of these doctrines have been thought essential to Christian faith by most fundamentalists.

## VALUABLE SERVICES OF FUNDAMENTALISM

Even in its original form, fundamentalism represented some important values and made significant contributions to Christian thought and life. In all these values the new evangelicalism participates, although some significant differences must be mentioned.

1. The fundamentalists continued a stress on Bible study and on the biblical message through times when the Bible was being widely neglected. All the distinctive symbols, appeal, and power of the church

are derived from the Bible or have come to us through that historical stream which has its source in the events reported in the Bible. Above all, it is from the Bible that we learn of Jesus Christ, without whom there is certainly no *Christian* and no *Christian church*. To be sure, Christ may be known in present religious experience as living Lord. However, even our religious experience and the image we form of Christ must be corrected by the Gospel record, lest in time we be so self-deceived that the Lord we preach be only the projection of our culture and not the true Savior by whom every culture must be judged and redeemed.

2. Insistence by the fundamentalists upon clarity and directness of theological affirmation was needed and is still needed, in days when some theologians seem more concerned with erecting impregnable defenses of obscurity than with sounding a clear call to which Christians can rally. Sometimes the conservatives have oversimplified matters. But the first function of language is to be understood; and fundamentalists have rendered real service, even to those who have differed radically, by setting up some well-established theological landmarks as points of reference.

3. The fundamentalists have stressed man's imperative need of God. In days of rapidly expanding scientific discovery and technical invention, to great human benefit, it has been especially easy to forget that "except the Lord build the house, they labor

in vain that build it" (Psalm 127:1). Yet events have shown that human skill destroys houses more rapidly than it builds and military "security" may produce the most abysmal insecurity. It is well that when the crises of World War II and the subsequent critical years came, our people had not forgotten to consider the judgments of God and to call upon him in time of trouble. In keeping Americans reminded of their absolute dependence upon God, even through proud, peaceful, and prosperous years, our more conservative churches did more than their share.

4. They have maintained the doctrine of a personal God, a Father with whom we can communicate in prayer, a Father purposively concerned with our human need. Much recent teaching has presented God in such impersonal or ambiguous terms as to raise the most serious doubt about the possibility of prayer and of God's love.

5. They have focused attention on the dimension of divine revelation and redeeming action in the life, death, and resurrection of Christ. Too often, liberals have made of the gospel, which originally meant "good news," simply good news of *man*, showing, in Jesus, what man could become. If this hope is to be fulfilled, we need also good news of *God*, of his purpose, his love, his power to redeem and save us.

6. They have taught the urgency of unequivocal decision for Christ, in times of sophisticated in-

decision and paralyzing gradualism. Liberals have tended to say that what individuals needed was gradual nurture. This gradualism is often an excuse for procrastination and irresponsibility.

7. Finally, the fundamentalists have cultivated among millions of Americans the practical piety of earnest personal prayer, world-wide evangelical concern, generous giving, and warm Christian fellowship. These are all good. It is no secret that churches with less conservative theological teaching have found it difficult to match the enthusiasm for practical piety generated in the churches of the fundamentalists and evangelicals.

## OBJECTIONS TO FUNDAMENTALISM AND EVANGELICALISM

Over against the values observed, we must place in consideration some objections to the conservative movements in Protestantism, as viewed by other Christians.

1. First is a biblicism which looks to many other Christians like an idolatry of the Book. To the Book itself, its printed page and its every word, is sometimes attributed such supernatural infallibility and power as most other Protestant Christians would attribute only to the living God himself. The Bible is the testimony by Israel and the Christian church to God's personal revelation to his people. By the early Christians the Book was treasured

because it preserved the memory of him who in his own person revealed God. This interpretation of the historical relationships and limitations of the Bible is less sharply opposed to the new evangelical theology than to the older fundamentalism.

2. Closely connected with biblicism is biblical literalism. Far too often verses have been strung together with reckless disregard of their meaning in the original contexts, in order to produce the appearance of proof for certain doctrines. Such argument has often been used despite abundant biblical teaching contrary to the propositions defended. These procedures are frequently denounced by the more scholarly fundamentalists, and even more by the new evangelicals. However, the doctrine of infallibility—even as taught by Carnell and Van Til—still opens the way for such "proof-texting" procedures.[12]

3. The conservatives of whom we have been speaking, it is charged, tend to neglect the humanity of Jesus Christ, falling into the ancient docetic or Apollinarian heresies. Jesus is then placed outside man's earthly, historical predicament. This is one reason why the saving relationship of Christ to the human being is usually depicted by fundamentalists as having to do principally with an otherworldly situation after death, with scant relation to our present economic, political, and social responsibilities.

4. It seems to many other Christians that the

fundamentalists seriously overemphasize the relative importance of ideational and even verbal conformity. The Christian life is thus made to appear mainly as an intellectual acceptance of certain beliefs and as a habit of repeating frequently certain phrases. Not only does such emphasis restrict freedom to search openly for more truth; it also places such a premium on formal and external conformity as to invite insincerity and to neglect the all-embracing wholeness of Christian living.

5. The stress on rigid conformity encourages the harsh, arrogant condemnation of all who differ. It is principally under fundamentalist leadership that there have arisen the worst movements expressing religious and racial intolerance and even hate, in recent American history. Many conservative religious leaders who themselves abhor such developments nevertheless encourage them by the proud and intolerant spirit of their dogmatic preaching. If the open-mindedness of liberalism tends to encourage easygoing evasion and intellectual aloofness, the dogmatic assurance of fundamentalism leads similarly to intolerance and self-righteous pride.

6. Ironically, while rigidly opposing any accommodation to modern culture as it relates to certain formulas of belief, and sometimes teaching resistance to such trivial private cultural expressions as the use of cosmetics and playing cards, fundamentalists generally acquiesce easily to the larger social

evils of the day. Militaristic belligerency, race prejudice, exploitation of natural resources, and industrial injustice are easily accepted or even defended by most of the theological conservatives, today, in contrast to the passion for freedom, equality, and brotherhood in the revivals of the mid-nineteenth century.

7. Fundamentalists, it is often said, have overstressed evangelistic revivals at the expense of Christian nurture. They have been right in insisting that gradual education is not enough; we need also hours of forthright challenge and decision. However, so extreme and one-sided is the stress on conversion, that in many churches every sermon is a new call to conversion and all church work is devoted to the winning of converts. Hence, it is complained, there is little opportunity for the people to grow morally and spiritually.

8. Finally, the fundamentalist commitment to certain teachings of an outmoded science has been extremely costly to the whole Christian movement. There are great numbers of American young people who have wanted earnestly to be Christians. Fundamentalist preachers or parents have told them that if they were to be Christians they must disbelieve biological evolution, accept the demonic causation of disease and accept every word of the Bible "from cover to cover." Many such young people have sadly faced the hard dilemma of being intellectually honest, on the one hand, or Christian,

on the other. Many conservatives would remind us
that in the first century, too, many learned men
found their "wisdom" incompatible with the Christian gospel. But less conservative churchmen say
that it will be a long time before American Protestantism fully recovers from the loss of honest and
intellectually superior leadership through the posing
of this tragic dilemma.

## FUNDAMENTALISM AND THE WIDER FELLOWSHIP

Many Christians of other persuasions frankly
acknowledge a certain wistfulness with which they
view the enthusiasm and devotion shown by many
fundamentalists. These earnest conservatives often
have a conviction and passion which others greatly
need. At the same time, such objections as have been
described may indicate that fundamentalists might
have something to gain from other Christians.
Their own professions of Christian love should lead
them more generously to seek fellowship with non-
fundamentalists. At the same time, the liberal professions of many other Christians should lead to a
more open-minded and charitable attitude toward
their more conservative Christian brothers. Few developments could be more promising of good than
the establishment of real, continual communication
between fundamentalists and the new evangelicals,
on the one hand, and the members of various diver-
gent movements, on the other.

## NOTES

1. Vols. 1-12. Chicago: Testimony Publishing Co., 1910-1914.
2. For a historical study of the whole movement, especially of its most influential years, see Norman F. Furniss, *The Fundamentalist Controversy, 1918-1931* (New Haven: Yale University Press, 1954).
3. For the most influential fundamentalist attack on evolution, see William Jennings Bryan, *In His Image* (New York: Fleming J. Revell Co., 1922).
4. Two books by the ablest fundamentalist scholars defending the doctrine of the Virgin Birth are J. Gresham Machen, *The Virgin Birth of Christ* (New York: Harper & Brothers, 1930) and James Orr, *The Virgin Birth of Christ* (New York: Charles Scribner's Sons, 1924).
5. See his *Christian Theology*, 3 vols. (Kansas City, Mo.: Nazarene Publishing Co., 1940).
6. See Van Til's long Introduction to Benjamin B. Warfield, *The Inspiration and Authority of the Bible*, ed. by Samuel G. Craig (Philadelphia: Presbyterian and Reformed Publishing Co., 1948) and Edward John Carnell, *An Introduction to Christian Apologetics, a Philosophic Defense of the Trinitarian-Theistic Faith* (Grand Rapids: William B. Eerdmans Publishing Co., 1948). Carnell's views are further liberalized in his later book, *The Case for Orthodox Theology* (Philadelphia: The Westminster Press, 1959).
7. The best-known eminent scholar among the early fundamentalists, J. Gresham Machen, wrote the most widely used introductory textbook in New Testament Greek, even now a standard work in colleges and divinity schools. See *New Testament Greek for Beginners* (New York: The Macmillan Company, 1923).

8. *Introduction to Christian Apologetics*, pp. 192-193.
9. Grand Rapids: William B. Eerdmans Publishing Co., 1947.
10. Nashville, Tenn.: Abingdon Press, 1957.
11. Philadelphia: Presbyterian and Reformed Publishing Co., 1946, 1953.
12. Carnell's further modification of his views, mentioned in note 6, above, will go far toward discouraging such practice. Those who accept his new position can claim decisive proof by citation of a text, only when quoting from Romans, for Carnell claims a higher authority for Romans and Galatians than for any other biblical writing, and places Romans above Galatians.

# CHAPTER FOUR

# EXISTENTIALISM

Existentialism is the belief that the truth most worth having is not grasped by objective knowledge or carefully defined ideas, but by a man's own passionately involved existence. Whereas scientists and most philosophers exhort us to seek truth by detached, dispassionate objectivity, the existentialists direct us rather to subjectivity, to taking sides, to living life in its full-blooded depths. Objective knowledge, they insist, is abstract, speculative, and, so far as the most basic questions of our personal existence are concerned, impossible. If we seek answers to our ultimate questions by rational investigation, we shall only withdraw further and further from the reality we seek to know. That reality cannot be "known" in the scientific sense, for our concepts can apprehend only essences, not existence. Existence, however, can be encountered and apprehended by faith.

This strange philosophy which would end philosophy in the traditional sense had its modern origin in the work of the Danish Christian thinker Sören Aabye Kierkegaard (1813-1855). A young contemporary in Russia, Fedor M. Dostoevski (1821-1881), expressed kindred themes in his powerful novels. The German atheist philosopher, Friedrich W. Nietzsche (1844-1900) was in many ways similar. All three men were protesting against the conventional self-deception and superficial idealization of grim reality in the new industrial society. They went further and struck out against every theoretical and practical effort to impose what appeared to them artificial structures on the untamed, creative, and terrible freedom of the human spirit. Between World War I and World War II, when the depth of man's predicament had been made plain, their influence came belatedly into its own. The German Martin Heidegger and the French patriot Jean-Paul Sartre would both dismiss traditional religion and traditional types of philosophy as among the despised artificialities. Martin Buber, a Jew, and Karl Jaspers, a theist unattached to institutional religion, sound authentic existentialist notes, though they are not typical. Among Christian theologians, the Russian Orthodox—but not so orthodox—layman Nicolas Berdyaev, the Roman Catholic Gabriel Marcel, and the Protestants Rudolf Bultmann and Paul Tillich represent a wide variety of existentialist interests and themes.

*suffering — desire — reason —*

## Sören Kierkegaard

Sören Kierkegaard inherited from his father high intelligence, sufficient money to provide a living until the year of his death, an earnest Christian piety, and a melancholy disposition. He loved Regina Olsen and his love was returned. Yet he was convinced that God required their engagement to be broken. He was called to an abnormal, suffering life of protest, burdened heavily with a sense of guilt which he believed other men were too conventional and superficial to feel.

The true Christian gospel, as he understood it, challenged everything in man's worldly existence and demanded unconditional surrender. The Danish church had so domesticated Christianity as to make nearly everyone a "Christian," without sacrifice, suffering, or any kind of break with the ways of the world. All Kierkegaard's writing is a declaration of the infinite qualitative distinction between time and eternity, man and God, and even between natural man, in all his thought and life, and the Christian, in whom the natural man—reason and all—has been crucified. He was therefore in the sharpest conflict with the church, with philosophy—especially that of the popular and pretentious Hegel—and with everyone who might try to make peace between the Christian faith and modern culture.

His teaching divides human life into three levels. The *aesthetic* is the life of immediate fulfillment and satisfaction. Kierkegaard's vivid descriptions of it show that he feels keenly its strong attractions. Not only art, music, and cultured society, but even the common pleasures of childhood and of simple life stir in him deep longings. Yet he knows well that man is not an animal. We cannot escape the demands of conscience and principle. When we recognize, with Socrates, that "the unexamined life is not worth living," and accept the rule of solemn duty, we move to the next higher level, which is the *ethical*. Here reason is guide, as we formulate moral principles and draw all kinds of practical inferences from them. In the end, however, Kierkegaard believes this effort at rational self-rule to be self-defeating. It is no less futile if, in the name of reason, a man postulates the existence of God as the final judge and arbiter of duty. A god accepted on such terms is only the projection of a man's own reason, in a religion which is essentially idolatrous self-worship. Besides, when man tries to apply objective rational methods for the solution of basic problems concerning his own existence, he only deceives himself, for every shred of his being is involved and he has no part of himself left to look on in detached, judicious appraisal of evidence. In any event, attempted objectivity directs his attention away from existence, which is always particular, to essence, which is always universal and abstract.

The only solution for a man's existential plight comes by recognition of his own sinful, helpless condition. When he is reduced to the utter despair which is true insight, he may be addressed by the eternal contemporary, Christ, the Paradox, in whom God crossed the gulf which no man can cross, became man and died for our redemption. When we confront Christ, it will be fatal to seek reasons for believing in him. To our sin-infected, defensive reason, Christ is sure to be an offense. Our only hope is to make a desperate, passionate decision of faith. To man's reason such an act of self-denial is impossible, but with God all things are possible. The faith which is man's supremely human act of decision is also a miraculous gift of God's grace.

## PAUL TILLICH

The most conspicuous existentialist thinker in the United States is German-born Paul Tillich. Radically unlike Kierkegaard, both in temperament and thought, he nevertheless shares the protest against the effort to understand our existence in exclusively conceptual terms, against conventional Western culture, and against the liberal effort to ally idealistic philosophy with the Christian faith.

"Religion means being ultimately concerned,"[1] says Tillich. This is a thought which he has emphasized in many ways. Much so-called religious art, he insists, is actually "dangerously irreligious."[2] It purports to present portraits of Jesus or of the Madonna and Child, but the figures shown are of people who fit easily into the life of an indifferent humanity. It portrays attractive persons of ordinary character, and with nothing to jar the observer's contentment with the pleasant world in which he fancies himself to live. Such art does not convey an ultimate concern and hence is not truly religious.

Likewise, Tillich insists, talks and sermons about God or Jesus or salvation may not be religious. Since the ultimate questions of our existence have not been asked, the historic answers to such questions are deprived of their meaning. The conservative churches have generally rested content with giving the traditional answers without taking time to show how the questions rise from the depths of our present situation. The old dogmas which once set hearts aflame are now repeated in smug complacency, while neither speakers nor hearers sense the relevance of the historic symbols to present existence. The liberals, on the other hand, emasculate the Christian symbols by defining their meaning in terms easily harmonizing with our present culture.

A more realistic appraisal of recent history, art, and philosophy, Tillich believes, will disclose to a sensitive soul the abysmal depths of man's estrangement from his own rightful essence. It is the task of the philosopher to make such disclosure, thus formulating with ultimate concern the questions to which revelation gives answer. This responding of revelation to philosophy Tillich calls the "method of correlation."[3] Employing such a method, he undertakes to produce a system of Christian theology which is both apologetic and kerygmatic, that is, which both commends the Christian faith to this age and is true to the significance of the original, revealed Christian message.

In positive statement of the Christian answers, Tillich makes much use of "symbol" and "myth" (a special kind of symbol). The traditional Christian affirmations are supported, but not as literal statements. They are to be understood symbolically, that is, as mediating between us and ultimate realities incapable of precise account in rational concepts. Even such Christian teachings as the doctrine of the resurrection of Christ, the life of believers after death, and the belief that God is spirit, are to be taken symbolically, not literally, although the doctrine that God is spirit is "the most embracing, direct, and unrestricted symbol for the divine life."[4] It can be asserted literally that "God is being-itself or the absolute. However, after this has been said, nothing else can be said about God as God which is not symbolic."[5] When we address God in an ego-thou relation, as is proper, we should understand that we are speaking symbolically. God is not literally a "Thou" to be addressed. God is the being-itself of all being, including ourselves.[6] Tillich stresses so much the "Logos"—the rationally structured, hence intelligible aspect—of God, that much he has to say is in the main tradition of European philosophy and contrary to typical existentialist emphasis. However, the "Abyss" is also of God, indeed makes Him truly God; and the Abyss is intrinsically beyond our understanding. Here the existentialist protest against conceptual limitations finds place even in the highly rational structure of Tillich's system.

Christ is the New Being in whom, we affirm by faith, existence has not been estranged from essence. His victory gives us hope that our own estrangement from our essential nature can be overcome. To appropriate this victory, a man "must accept that he is accepted; he must accept acceptance."[7] This is the meaning of justification by grace through faith, and by it a man is reconciled to the being-itself of his own being and of all being, that is, to God.

## OTHER EXISTENTIALISTS

No branch of Christendom has a body of formal doctrine more firmly placed dogmatically beyond question or change than Eastern Orthodoxy. Yet one of the most widely and appreciatively read Christian thinkers of recent times is the Russian Orthodox layman, Nicolas Berdyaev. One reason this is possible is that changeless dogmas are understood mystically and interpreted with spiritual flexibility in the Eastern churches.

The dominant motifs of Berdyaev's life and writ-

ing were passion for freedom, concern for the dignity of man, and the conviction that in God was to
be found the fulfillment of both. Throughout his
work these interests were affected by a deep strain
of mysticism especially characteristic of Russian
Orthodoxy.

In some respects Berdyaev is the very opposite of
Kierkegaard. Instead of a vast gulf between man
and God, he sees the most intimate union, of which
Christ, the God-man, is symbol. Our state of slavery to the world alone separates us from the very
roots of our own being in the universal Spirit of
God. In this Berdyaev is more like Tillich. He is also
like Tillich in interpreting the historic creeds symbolically. On the other hand, he exalts personality
as an ultimate category, even the most meaningful
category of all. Because God and man are both personal, all their relations must be conceived in
personal terms, not in the abstract concepts of
impersonal ontology nor of institutional government. "Personality allows only of correlation,
meeting, communion. And God as personality does
not desire a man over whom he can rule, and who
ought to praise him, but man as personality, who
answers His call and with whom the communion of
love is possible."[8]

Strikingly similar to Berdyaev in his emphasis on
the personal and his protest against every practical
or theoretical tendency to depersonalize man or God
is Karl Jaspers. In his later years he has rejected

the earlier influence of Kierkegaard toward a depreciation of reason and, in his book *Reason and Anti-reason in Our Time*,[9] has vigorously defended the rational quest of truth. However, it is undeniable that he arrived at his own form of personalism by way of the existentialist protest against every tendency to subordinate human freedom to other forces or philosophical categories.

Even Roman Catholic thought has not escaped being influenced by the existentialist movement. Indeed, the neo-Thomist Etienne Gilson has tried to establish the idea that St. Thomas Aquinas was an existentialist![10] However, despite disclaimers, this must be regarded as a pedagogic and apologetic device, rather than a classification which can be taken seriously. To be sure, St. Thomas was existentialist in the sense that he was mainly concerned with the most basic problems of existence itself and intended to live by the truth he learned and taught. In that sense, we must add, every serious metaphysician has been an existentialist. If existentialism is defined in a way to distinguish it as a particular philosophical movement, then St. Thomas is one of the best examples of the kind of philosophy *against* which existentialism is a protest. Certainly, St. Thomas believed that men could know the truth about God, the world and themselves by objective, scientifically precise reason. To be sure, like nearly all other rational philosophers, he believed that reason must use data provided from some source other than itself. In his case such data were purportedly drawn from sense perception for philosophy and from revelation for theology.

Actually, other assumptions were employed also, among them the essentially impersonal categories of Aristotle. The Thomistic proofs and definitions of God as unmoved mover, first cause, necessary being, most perfect being, and even supreme intelligence, would be far from satisfactory to any of the modern existentialists. It is precisely this sort of objective effort at conceptual definition and proof of God which is the philosophical object of their most emphatic protest. However, Gilson retorts that the protest is wrongly directed. Only the Thomists know how to solve the basic problem attacked in vain by such modern existentialists as Kierkegaard, Heidegger, and Jaspers. "As philosophy of the act-of-being," he writes, "Thomism is not *another* existential philosophy, it is the only one."[10]

Gilson's principal contributions are in his remarkable studies of medieval thought. His long life of scholarship has been devoted to the task of calling philosophy and theology back to St. Thomas, rather than contributing new philosophical or theological ideas. Indeed, he warns against efforts to improve on the system of St. Thomas, "fixed as it is by its very perfection."[11]

Other neo-Thomists such as Martin D'Arcy, and especially Jacques Maritain, have contributed much more of pioneering thought. D'Arcy, besides his persuasive Roman Catholic apologetics, has contributed effectively to basic Christian ethics. Maritain has a well-deserved philosophical reputation, especially for his liberal contributions to social and political thought.

Radically different is the teaching of such a Roman Catholic as Gabriel Marcel. He does not attack the dogma of the Church, but thinks in ways diverging far from the methods of St. Thomas. His categories are drawn from psychology, music, art, and drama. He uses them, not as concepts to be ever more sharply defined, but as symbols purposefully suggestive and serving as guides to the kind of self-understanding, release of creative imagination, and voluntary social commitment which enable man to be truly man. Some questions which we confront, Marcel maintains, are not capable of being conceptually answered, as problems are solved, but must rather be lived with, ever more profoundly, as infinite mysteries. Here again is the authentic existentialist protest against the attempt to grasp all reality in precisely definable concepts, even though Marcel has disavowed the existentialist label.

One more Protestant existentialist must be discussed briefly. Rudolf Bultmann is best known for his radical form criticism in New Testament studies. He reduces much of the material in the Gospels to certain discernible types or forms of testimony in which mythical symbols of the times have large place. Since the myths of the first-century church were characteristic of ancient Jewish and Hellenic culture, but are foreign to our own ways of thinking, we must "demythologize" the Gospels before we can learn the real substance of their teaching. Critical historical study, according to Bultmann, shows that Jesus was a man who claimed no messiahship for himself, but pointed to another who was to come as Son of Man. He shared one form of the popular and misguided apocalypticism of his day. After his crucifixion some of his disciples concluded that Jesus himself was the heavenly Son of Man whose coming he foretold and that he would come again, in power and glory. However, God made this common man the one in whom the Incarnation took place. Jesus and the primitive church's faith in him together constitute the Event we call Jesus Christ. This Event is God's Eternal Word of Salvation. It is this paradoxical faith in the Incarnation in a common man who was crucified which the gospel demands that we accept. The fact that we do not find such faith reasonable is nothing against it, for what seems like foolishness to man's proud and sinful reason is the highest wisdom of God, though God is not to be regarded as literally purposive. Bultmann's thought is thus a remarkable combination of rational, objectively critical historical studies, from which considerations of the powerful faith of the Christian movement are excluded, and, on the other hand, an abrupt, defiant affirmation of personal, paradoxical faith.

## CONTRIBUTIONS OF EXISTENTIALISM

1. The existentialists have served to remind us of the nonrational aspects of our experience and of the Christian faith. God, the world, and even the depths of our own being present mysteries which scientists and objective philosophers are in danger of ignoring because they resist their methods of analysis and definition.

2. By their use of myth and symbol, the existentialists have enabled many honest and thoughtful men to repudiate literal interpretations of some ancient dogmas, while retaining their imagery and suggestiveness to thought as guides to deep meditation and the worship of God. Fortunately for us, it is possible to know God in prayer without adequate formulation of doctrine about him. Tillich has been especially helpful to many people in emancipating the spirit from dogmas to which they could not honestly subscribe, while provoking that ultimate concern without which no doctrines have truly religious value.

3. Kierkegaard, especially, has impressed upon us again the truth that we are saved by faith and not by reasoning. However helpful reason may be, if we are to live as God intended, there comes a moment when we must decide. In an age of widespread cultured urbanity in which indecision is made a virtue, Kierkegaard's flaming proclamation of the either/or, before which our whole existence

hangs upon our fateful decision, has rendered an inestimably great service.

4. The existentialists have, by their critique of reason, made it dramatically emphatic that all reasoning is dependent on some unproved postulates of faith. Man in his actual existence has a choice between faiths; he has not a choice between a rational life, on the one hand, and a life of faith on the other.

5. The passion for reality so dramatically and resourcefully expressed by a number of the existentialists serves to rout many a person out of his complacent contentment with mediocre conformity to secondhand ideas and send him on an ardent pilgrimage to God. There is no deadlier foe of genuine piety than a conventional parroting of other people's religious language and the easygoing conformity to respectable religious customs without serious personal concern. It may take the massive, foreboding realism of a Dostoevski or the anguished passion of a Kierkegaard to shock a smug conformist into realization of his need which no human device nor thought, but only God himself, can fulfill.

## SHORTCOMINGS OF EXISTENTIALISM

Important as have been the contributions of existentialism to Christian life and thought, Christians who think otherwise contend that it has shown certain characteristic exaggerations and weaknesses.

1. Some representatives of this movement, not content with showing the true limits of rational thought have encouraged a readiness to ignore or defy all rational considerations in the most important decisions of life. While a Kierkegaard may then choose the Paradox, Christ, a Heidegger may, for a time, choose Hitler; and a Sartre may commit himself as passionately both to the resistance against Hitler and to atheism. If all considerations of evidence are ruled out in advance, what is to guide our existence to reality, rather than to the most unrealistic madcap adventure next proposed to us? Jaspers himself has said of the man who embraces faith without reason, "By renouncing reason, he has without noticing the fact, renounced freedom. He is ready for any kind of totalitarianism and follows the ringleader to destruction, crime and a shameful death along with the rest of the herd."[12]

2. Though many persons are content with mediocre conformity and therefore need shock treatment, existentialism may, in the end, render a disservice by cultivating a taste for shrill screaming and lurid exaggeration. History offers small hope that the right solutions to our most urgent dilemmas will be found by people more concerned with exciting and extreme declamations than with evidences of truth and sobriety. Fanaticism has done enough damage already, without further encouragement from the scholarly world, to which men look for

guidance based on superior knowledge and disciplined thought.

3. Such reasonable men as Tillich, Marcel, and Jaspers have not contributed to the first two alleged evils of existentialist influence. However, they have shared in another, which seems inherent in the very nature of the movement. Through many centuries language has been refined and sharpened for communication of exact ideas. Much work in philosophy and the special sciences has been invested in this very task. Now, when words are deliberately employed in the form of cognitive affirmations but for noncognitive effects, as symbols, the resulting ambiguity of communication may border on irresponsible deception, sometimes self-deception. Is anything valuable to be gained by affirming belief in the resurrection when one actually believes that death is the end, or in addressing God as "Thou," when one honestly thinks God to be none other than the very being-itself of all being, including oneself? Much existentialist use of myth and symbol looks perilously like an effort to deny the meaning of the historic Christian doctrines, while seeking so to entertain them in imagination as to indulge the emotional effects of believing them.

4. Much existentialist thought moves on the very edge of antinomianism, that is, the repudiation of all moral law as related to salvation. Kierkegaard's depreciation of consistency and his doctrine that God commands the unethical and irrational, and

Tillich's defining of justification as "acceptance of acceptance," without specifying the need of repentance, tend to lessen the moral earnestness of Christian faith. Opponents of existentialism contend that in a world where God gives commands which are bound to seem absurd to human reason and where man is under no obligation to be consistent to principle, it might as well be true, precisely as Kierkegaard himself says, that "love to God may cause the knight of faith to give his love to his neighbor the opposite expression to that which, ethically speaking, is required by duty."[13] With such encouragement and all our human propensities to sin, it is asked, what safeguards have we against a new resurgence of every monstrous cruelty and villainy ever perpetrated in the name of religion?

5. One more charge against existentialist thought must be heard. Philosophically, existentialism is a skeptical movement. Whatever faith it asserts must be affirmed after previous efforts at constructive philosophy have been demolished. Doctrines previously taught as revealed, along with those often defended as rationally probable, are generally viewed with intellectual condescension or disapproval. The later return of these doctrines as myths or symbols still leaves the intellectual substance of belief vague and thin. It is sometimes hard to discover, through the haze of symbolic language, what the existentialist does believe is actually so. When we have discovered, we often find the real doctrine

but a pale shadow of the beliefs which have sustained the courage of the martyrs and the daily piety of toiling multitudes.

Is it possible to gain the great values offered by the existentialists without such an inflation of verbal, ideational, and emotional currency as to leave the recipient poorer, even, than before? Many explorations of such possibilities are in progress. Some of them will be encountered among the crisis theologians and others influenced by them. They will be our next subjects for study.

## NOTES

1. "Existentialist Aspects of Modern Art," in *Christianity and the Existentialists*, edited by Carl Michalson (New York: Charles Scribner's Sons, 1956), p. 132.
2. *Ibid.*, p. 142.
3. *Systematic Theology*, Vol. I (Chicago: University of Chicago Press, 1951), p. 59.
4. *Ibid.*, p. 249.
5. *Ibid.*, p. 239. In Vol. II, Tillich concedes that even the statement that God is being-itself is symbolic.
6. *Ibid.*, p. 271.
7. *Ibid.*, Vol. II (1957), p. 179.
8. *Slavery and Freedom* (New York: Charles Scribner's Sons, 1944), p. 40.
9. New Haven: Yale University Press, 1952.
10. Anton Pegis, editor, *A Gilson Reader* (Garden City, N.Y.: Doubleday & Company, Inc., 1957), p. 261. Cf *ibid.*, pp. 18, 206, 208, 256. Jacques Maritain has contrasted the "authentic existentialism" of St. Thomas with the "apocryphal existentialism, the current kind,"

in a carefully discriminating way. See his *Existence and the Existent* (Garden City, N.Y.: Doubleday & Company, Inc., 1957), p. 13 and *passim*.

11. *A Gilson Reader, opicit.,* p. 84.
12. *Reason and Anti-reason in Our time,* p. 76.
13. *Fear and Trembling,* published with *The Sickness unto Death* (Garden City, N.Y.: Doubleday & Company, Inc., 1955), p. 80.

# CHAPTER FIVE

# NEO-REFORMATION THEOLOGY

Like fundamentalism, neo-Reformation theology is a reaction against liberal accommodation to culture. However, neo-Reformation theology is more sophisticated, and it takes for granted some ideas stressed by the liberals but rejected by fundamentalists. Though fundamentalism seeks to return to a pre-liberal Christianity, neo-Reformation theology is intentionally postliberal.

The movement we are now discussing is more commonly known as neo-orthodoxy. *Neo-Reformation theology* is a preferable name for two reasons. First, it is more specific. A new "orthodoxy" could refer to the orthodoxy of the Eastern Orthodox churches, of Roman Catholicism, or of any other long-established tradition. The thinkers with whom we are now concerned seek quite specifically to restore certain emphases which they take to be the authentic and essential doctrines of the Protestant Reformers, especially Martin Luther and John Calvin. The neo-Reformation theologians should be distinguished from the Roman Catholic and Anglican leaders who seek to restore certain emphases of St. Thomas ("neo-Thomists"), the Methodists who revive characteristic teachings of John Wesley ("neo-Wesleyans"), and others who call for renewal of certain early Baptist doctrines. Second, in the heat of theological controversy, "neo-orthodoxy" has become increasingly established as a term of opprobrium. A term of such vaguely defined meaning lends itself especially easily to such emotionally charged usage. This is one reason why nearly all writers whom we should be inclined to call neo-orthodox disclaim the title or deprecate its vagueness.

Even when we use the clearer and more specific label, we continue to denote a wide variety of thinkers, some of whom have been involved in very vigorous and basic disagreement.

## KARL BARTH

There is no doubt that Karl Barth has made a stronger impact upon Protestant theology than any other man of the twentieth century, thus far. So varied and far-reaching is his influence that whether one welcomes his ideas or opposes them one cannot ignore them and still gain even an elementary understanding of the present situation in theology.

His early liberal and socially concerned preaching—much influenced by Albrecht Ritschl—failed to produce any noteworthy results among his discouraged and confused Swiss parishioners, during World War I. This failure led Barth to a radical re-examination of his doctrine in relation to the Bible. The result was a drastic change and a new, powerful voice of affirmation and protest.

No path of reasoning about our human experience can lead us to the knowledge of God, he now declared, nor can any amount of moral effort gain a life righteous and acceptable to God. God confronts man in judgment. We cannot gain either theoretical or practical familiarity with Him. He is the Other, before whom all our thinking and striving are under condemnation. The liberal thought of Schleiermacher and Ritschl stressed the continuity between the human and the divine. Our experiences of feeling and value joined us with God and formed a pathway by which we could enter, by thought and religious practice, into his presence. On the contrary, declares Barth, there is only discontinuity between us sinful men and the holy God. We cannot by any means cross the chasm which separates us. Only God can cross over it, as he speaks his word of self-disclosure, judgment, and redemption.

It soon became evident that such teaching had a close affinity with the thought of Kierkegaard, and

Barth gratefully acknowledged his indebtedness to the Danish existentialist. However, the further he developed his study of the Scriptures from the new standpoint, the less use he had for existentialist philosophy. Even this critical analysis of our human limitation and sin, he came to believe, was a needless and even dangerous excursion in human effort to find truth and salvation. Instead of learning, through existentialist analysis, to say "No" to all human self-affirmation independent of God, one should simply begin by listening to the word of God spoken in the Scriptures. There one would hear God's "No" of judgment, accompanied by his "Yes" of redeeming love.

Perhaps Barth saw that if a reader of existentialist philosophy experienced the shattered despair of reasoned knowledge and of salvation by human effort, he might simply remain in despair and so die, or he might make the leap of faith to accept some pseudosavior, like Marxism, instead of Christ. Better begin and end with the Word of God, finding the ground for both human despair and God-given hope in the same Christ. The Bible needs no philosophical preparation, whether existentialist or any other.

Barth denounces all natural theology, including all notions of natural law in the ethical sense. Man's reason cannot discover either God or human duty. Attempts at such discovery lead only to false gods which are projections of man's own conception, and to the idolatry of obedience to human reason rather than to the one true God.

All human interpretations of the revealing word of God are bound to be stammering, inconsistent, and inadequate. Theology can be coherent or clear, and can display an air of completeness or finality only by substituting human speculation for the shattering and, to man, confusing offense of the divine word. It is no accident that God's word comes with such staggering and disruptive effect. Sinful and finite man must be brought to his knees in complete distrust of himself and in utter reliance upon the one wholly other God if he is to be saved.

There could scarcely be a writer harder to summarize accurately in the few words which can be allotted even to so important a single theologian in a book like this. Barth affirms many theological propositions with staccato sharpness and explosive force, almost monotonously followed by exclamation points. But when the reader believes he has Barth's thought quite clearly in hand, he encounters modifying or even contrary assertions of similar force. The reader insistent on judging all he reads by canons of rational consistency, coherence, and empirical verifiability will write him off as an author of dramatically worded nonsense. But the Barthian enthusiasts will reply in the word of St. Paul that when truly preached, "Christ crucified" is always a stumbling-block to Jews and folly to Gentiles, but to those who are called, both Jews and Greeks, Christ the power of God and the wisdom of God. For the foolishness of God is wiser than men, and the weakness of God is stronger than men.[1]

In the history of Christian thought God has been declared both as transcendent, distant, mysterious, and also as immanent, near, well-known. Barth, like Calvin and Luther, but more than either, teaches that God is mysterious, hidden, and transcendent. The divine likeness in which man was created has been utterly obliterated by sin, so that there is nothing in human reason or experience by which we could know God. He has been revealed to us only in his own crossing of the chasm to us.

Consequently, theology and our faith itself must rest exclusively upon the Word of God, Jesus Christ, made known to us through "the Word as written" (scriptural testimony), "the Word as preached" (the church's total ministry in Christ's name), and "the Word as revealed." "The Word as revealed" occurred first in God's original acts of revelation to which the Bible is human, and hence fallible, testimony; and it occurs again when the Holy Spirit awakens a response of faith in the present hearer or reader of preached or written testimony.

Unlike Calvin, Barth contends that God has not predestined any men to eternal damnation. God's "No" of condemnation has been taken upon himself in Christ, while his "Yes" of salvation and blessedness is offered to all men in Christ. This does not guarantee that all men will, in fact, have faith and be saved, but it does mean that we view even the unbelief of men with hope, because we also see God's purpose in Christ. In any event, for this neo-Calvinist, Barth, "faith in God's predestination in itself and per se means faith in man's non-rejection, not faith in his rejection."[2]

God has won for us the victory over sin and death, in Jesus Christ. But we await the full manifestation of this victory in Christ's coming again. Meanwhile, "between the times," evil, though already dealt the death blow, continues on its way. We cannot stop it, and nothing we can do will in any way hasten the full manifestation of God's reign. This does not mean, however, that our plight is hopeless, for God has already done what was needful, in the death and resurrection of Christ. We now await, with faith and assurance, His full manifestation and glory.

As we wait, we pray, in obedience to God's will, and we work in obedient testimony of our faith in his grace by which we are saved. Our labors in the church, in daily work of farm, shop, or home, and in the social order, do not hasten the fulfillment of our hope. But they are necessary testimonies of grateful and obedient love. If we believe in Christ, we shall perform these works of love with gladness.

## EMIL BRUNNER

In the early days of Karl Barth's neo-Calvinist preaching, Emil Brunner was universally regarded as a colleague in the task of reforming the doctrine of the European Reformed and Lutheran churches. However, as both men continued to develop their thought with vigor and originality, their relationship became strained until, in a polemic booklet entitled *No!*[3] Barth sharply repudiated Brunner's position and refused his proffered hand of renewed friendly understanding.

The subject of dispute on which Barth broke with his old friend was the question of a "point of contact" in man at which God might encounter and address him. Barth flatly denied the existence of any such point whatever. He held that the slightest concession on this issue would open the way again to men's trust in something which they might do as offering something acceptable to God or useful for their knowledge and salvation. Brunner denied that he meant to affirm anything good in man, but insisted that God did address man as man and hence there must be in man at least some latent need or capacity, however overlaid, perverted, and hidden from men's own eyes, by sin. The material image of God had been destroyed, but the formal image of God remained.

Moreover, Brunner insisted, God presented to men a general revelation of himself in nature, which man was formally capable of understanding. Until saved by the grace of Christ, man perverts the knowledge of God so gained, and yet there is a vague, imperfect knowledge, nevertheless. A Christian, on the other hand, may rightly construct a natural theology by the use of the data which God has provided in his creation. To all this Barth says, "No!" To be sure, sinful man is still man, but he is absolutely powerless to give even the slightest assistance to God for his own salvation—even by any sort of vague or imperfect knowledge. There is no general revelation, but only revelation in Christ. Brunner, however, thinks the general revelation of God to be objectively given through creation, even though subjectively man does not receive it.

Since Barth's *No!* in 1934, Brunner has continued his own independent development. His doctrine of general revelation has enabled him to enter into serious discussion with people of various points of view, and so has brought him into more positive and wide communication with modern world culture. His wide travels, including extensive lectures in America and Japan, have further broadened his perspective. Often he enters into philosophical ethics and metaphysics on their own grounds.

Brunner continues to stress the transcendent sovereignty of God and the depravity of man, in authentic Calvinist fashion. At the same time he discusses the relation between revelation and reason in affirmative terms. He also stresses the "encounter" or "meeting" (the German *Begegnung*) between God and man in a manner not too far from the reaffirming of belief in religious experience, which Barth continues brusquely to reject. Both men continually appeal to the authority of the Bible, but Brunner acknowledges more candidly and carefully the limitations of this authority and gives a more measured interpretation. Brunner seeks to persuade the reader, and Barth's books read like series of proclamations.

## REINHOLD NIEBUHR

By comparison with Barth and Brunner, Reinhold Niebuhr has retained much more of liberal thought. He rejects Kierkegaard's antirationalism, but pays high tribute to his psychological insights into the nature and predicament of man. His practical interests, throughout his entire ministry, have been concentrated in political and economic reform. His theological interests have been concerned largely with the search for a more realistic and penetrating understanding of man and society, which might serve as a sound basis for social policy. His main concerns are with Christian ethics, the Christian understanding of history, and the Christian doctrine of man.[4]

He protests vigorously against the tendency of some liberals to equate "God" with universal law, with reason in general, or with any other abstract, rational conception. He agrees with the naturalists that the belief in God as a person is rationally absurd, but despite its absurdity he upholds precisely this belief, which he thinks an essential of the Christian faith. It is rationally absurd because the very idea of a personal being involves the idea of both structure and freedom, and no system of thought has been found which can do justice to both.

Similarly, he maintains that no systematic doctrine of man can properly acknowledge the contrary aspects of his reason, his causally determined nature, his freedom, and his bondage to sin. We should seek to make our thought as coherent as we can without sacrificing the full diversity and tension of experienced reality. However, when dealing with such subjects as the freedom of God or the sin of man, the myths of Scripture illuminate the realities much better than any conceptual scheme of thought.

A favorite theme, to which Niebuhr returns again and again, is man's propensity to assert the meaning of his existence by a proud grasping at power or wealth, thus sinning and so denying the true meaning of his existence. Man thus becomes burdened with a sense of guilt and insecurity, and so struggles the more desperately for worldly power. Even religion commonly becomes perverted to a sentimental shielding of this sinfulness, and the sin which is indulged by self-righteous piety is the most wretched of all. Such false piety is exemplified, on the one hand, by the self-righteous nationalistic prosecution of the international struggle for power. It is seen, on the other hand, in those pacifists who, standing immersed in the social advantages of their nation's superior power, think they can escape responsibility for war and even end war by the simple expedient of renouncing participation in war. Actually, Niebuhr believes, there is no real solution of our great social problems within history. The real solution will be enacted by God, beyond history. Yet within history it is our obligation of faith to love our neighbors, in personal relations, and to seek such proximate justice as can be attained, in public affairs.

## THE WIDER MOVEMENT

Many other theologians have recently sought, in various ways, to restore characteristic emphases of the Protestant Reformation, while maintaining critical studies of biblical history and literature. Among them must be mentioned the Swedish Lutheran theologians of Lund, Gustaf Aulén, with his historical study of the Cross[5] and his moderately Lutheran system of Christian doctrine,[6] and Anders Nygren, who launched a long and fruitful discussion of Christian love.[7] Most scholarly theologians in Germany are either existentialists or neo-Reformation thinkers or both. Hendrik Kraemer has applied the new theology to the development of a theology of missions.[8] Joseph L. Hromadka has borne a difficult witness in Communist-ruled Czechoslovakia.

British theology has been much affected by this movement, though tending to moderate its more extreme aspects. T. F. Torrance of Scotland ably defends a Calvinism much influenced by Barth. Leonard Hodgson is best known for ably defending a social view of the Trinity.[9]

In America, Edwin Lewis reacted strongly against his early cautious venture into moderate liberalism and has since represented, on the whole, a Methodist type of neo-orthodoxy, though with frequent indication, in the later years, of the more open-minded quest earlier in evidence. Joseph Haroutunian and Paul Lehmann ably defend neo-Calvinism in America. Paul S. Minear combines a keen and radical use of historical criticism in New Testament studies, with a conservative interpretation of most biblical themes. Many others should be mentioned.

A movement so varied is difficult to characterize summarily and accurately. Yet there are certain tendencies which, in various degrees, are to be found wherever it has gained prominence. In general, the neo-Reformation theology accepts biblical criticism, but stresses biblical authority; condemns liberal optimism about human nature and history, and dwells on the sinful nature of fallen man; depreciates philosophy and all attempts to press rational criteria of truth in matters of faith; speaks much of the hidden, mysterious, transcendent nature of God, denying or minimizing his immanence; condemns "pietism" and "moralism" among Christians, and emphasizes our exclusive dependence on Christ's righteousness, not our own.

## CONTRIBUTIONS OF NEO-REFORMATION THEOLOGY

Even among Christian thinkers who have continually resisted this movement, many would gladly concede that it has contributed some important correctives and other values to the Christian church. Among these values may be included those below.

1. Certainly, such men as Barth, Brunner, and Reinhold Niebuhr have immeasurably increased interest in theology. Some readers have been angered by them, while some have idolized them, but few have been able to remain indifferent. The sharply provocative challenge which neo-Reformation theology has thrown down to prevalent ways of thinking has made theology exciting and popular. The great number of able minds now working hard on studies in this field augurs well for the future both of theology and of the church. Many of them were stirred to these studies by theologians of the type we have been examining.

2. Through this movement interest in the Bible has been greatly increased. If the salutary message of the Bible is to be received, it must be heard and read. College and seminary professors and book-

sellers, alike, can testify to a great recent resurgence of Bible reading and Bible study, partially due to neo-Reformation theology.

3. Not only is the Bible being studied more than in the earlier decades of this century; it is being studied as possessing authoritative directives to life. Though the conservatives have been teaching, all along, that the Bible had such authority, great numbers of educated people who could not honestly believe that the biblical words were true "from cover to cover," have been deeply stirred by the more discriminating and imaginative, yet powerfully affirmative doctrines of the new "biblical theology."

4. Liberal preaching and education tended to encourage a belief in slow, gradual improvement, which often tempted people to rest on the assumption that since any good thing would take time there was no urgent need for decisive commitment. Neo-Reformation theology, by its stress on discontinuity and the seriousness of man's plight, has been for many a useful corrective of easy indecision.

5. This theological movement has emphasized that all men stand guilty under the judgments of God. It is necessary that the judgment of God be acknowledged if we are to escape the complacency and moral relativism which threaten our very humanity. Without belief in the judgment of God, belief in his love becomes an insipid sentimentality.

6. In the face of a subtle but often real transfer of attention, even in the churches, from God to human skill and effort, neo-Reformation theology has reasserted in emphatic terms the centrality of God. The recognition of this centrality would be acknowledged by most Christians as absolutely necessary to the Christian faith.

7. Some of the theologians we have been discussing, especially Reinhold Niebuhr, have given many vigorous and salutary warnings against the adoption of oversimplified, legal solutions of social problems as "the Christian solutions." Such identification of Christian objectives with proposals of reform, at best historically dated and at worst ill-conceived and disastrous in consequence, has often brought the gospel into undeserved ill-repute and produced the ugliest kind of partisan selfrighteousness.

8. When some congregations, especially in America, were convinced that they could live their petty lives in comfortable familiarity with God, the new reformers have served to remind many that the true God is transcendently great and holy, surpassing all that we can imagine or clearly conceive. This reminder has made it possible for many to bow before Him for the first time in genuine reverence and awe. Without the inclusion of such attitudes, religion is trivial and false.

## CHARACTERISTIC TEMPTATIONS AND NEGLECTS

Opponents say that like other historical movements of great usefulness, the neo-Reformation theology carries with it the temptation to exaggerate its virtues into such excesses as to make of them vices. The dramatic and highly polemic character of this theology, indeed, makes it peculiarly liable to such temptation and to the neglect of truths which do not seem particularly useful to its controversial interests. Some of the more plausible of these charges against neo-Reformation theology must now be specified.

1. This theology came into being in such a broadside against the dominant themes of modern culture that it has been tempted to loose generalization, hence inaccurate history and indiscriminate attack. Thus, when Barth attacks Brunner as holding a position implying that he is about to join "the Romanists,"[10] or Niebuhr describes liberal theology as reducing the sacrificial love expressed at Calvary "to the dimensions of simple mutuality,"[11] the result is a caricature, hardly worthy of scholarly search for truth. There have been too many such instances. Perhaps those advocates are correct who say they would not have been heard without such dramatic exaggerations. Yet it remains to be said that a price has been paid for the attention thus secured and accounts ought soon to be balanced. It must be added that dramatic exaggeration has

come to be so favorite a device among some of the younger theologians that for them truth seems secondary to excitement.[12]

2. The insistence that some mysteries of the gospel are suprarational and that the truth is paradoxical tends to encourage loose method and assertion unsupported by critical application of rational principles. Paradox can be a powerful stimulus to hard search for consistency beyond the paradox. But when one settles down, content with inconsistency, the way is opened to both theoretical and practical irresponsibility.

3. The use of paradox, the affirmations of doctrines in the form of symbol and myth, and the striving for dramatic and edifying effect have all tended toward equivocal and vaguely defined use of words. For example, a theologian who uses these devices may condemn the doctrine of immortality as a "pagan Greek" idea, and insist on the "true Christian" doctrine of "the resurrection of the body." This may sound ultra-orthodox, until the careful reader discovers that "the resurrection of the body" is called a symbolic myth which purportedly asserts a truth too profound for conceptual statement. What, then, does the myth symbolize? A future life of the individual after death? Absorption of the individual in God? The ongoing life of creatures on this earth? Or an unspecified hope for the future? In the interest of honesty and clarity, the

critics say, such equivocation should be rooted out of theological usage.

4. A mood which disparages human effort and points all hope toward God produces many churchmen who find little motivation or guidance for any human effort to solve or ameliorate the problems of our earthly society. Reinhold Niebuhr has repeatedly pointed out this defect in what he calls the "irresponsible eschatology" of Karl Barth, despite Barth's own social action. Some of Niebuhr's own readers, though granting his more predictable and constant social action, complain that they find little more help from him in their search for clear, guiding, ethical principles or basic ethical motivation.

5. Neo-Reformation theology is largely devoted to criticizing and correcting other schools of thought. Many of its advocates deny the propriety of any attempt to construct systems of theology. Indeed, it is questionable whether a system, in the strict sense, can be constructed without taking consistency and systematic method more seriously than most theologians of the neo-Reformation movement are prone to take them. If the Christian church is to have systems of doctrine upon which to base Christian instruction, church policy, and its intellectual encounter with the world, will it not need to move beyond a mood of compensatory reaction and dramatic exaggeration to a patient, critical reconstruction of thought?

6. The strong emphasis on discontinuity between

revelation and reason and between the gospel and culture tends to weaken communication between Christian testimony and the world. The result, it is often complained, is especially serious in the university. If the best which the theologian can do is to utter pronouncements, then he will have little influence on developments in philosophy, psychology, education, or the law. Effective communication in the intellectual community must be two-way communication, with willingness to adopt the language of our common culture and to learn as well as teach. Karl Barth and a number of other theologians deny the propriety of any intellectual defense of Christian faith. But the practical needs of the Christian world mission require such defense. Christians must be ready to give reasons for their faith and reasons why others should share it. The Christian church has always required rational apologetics. Is there good reason to think that such a discipline is no longer needed?

## NOTES

1. I Corinthians 1:23-25 (RSV).
2. *Kirchliche Dogmatik*, Vol. II, p. 182; as translated by Arthur C. Cochrane and quoted by Otto Weber, in *Karl Barth's Church Dogmatics* (Philadelphia: The Westminster Press, 1953), p. 97. In Vol. III, 1, some of Barth's statements seem unequivocally to affirm universal salvation.
3. *No! Answer to Emil Brunner*, in *Natural Theology*, John Baillie, ed. (London: Geoffrey Bles, The Centenary Press, 1946).

4. See especially his Gifford Lectures, *The Nature and Destiny of Man* (New York: Charles Scribner's Sons, 1941, 1953).

5. *Christus Victor* (New York: The Macmillan Company, 1951).

6. *The Faith of the Christian Church* (Philadelphia: Muhlenberg Press, c. 1948).

7. *Agape and Eros*, 3 volumes (New York: The Macmillan Company, 1932-1938).

8. See *The Communication of the Christian Faith* (Philadelphia: The Westminster Press, 1956).

9. See *The Doctrine of the Trinity* (London: Nisbet and Co., 1943).

10. *No!* P. 85, *op. cit.* in note 3.

11. *Christian Realism and Political Problems* (New York: Charles Scribner's Sons, 1953), p. 190.

12. For a strong defense of a very moderate Neo-Reformation theology, see William Hordern, *The Case for a New Reformation Theology* (Philadelphia: The Westminster Press, 1959).

# CHAPTER SIX

# OLD AND NEW
# AGREEMENTS

Our discussions have had to do with so many points of opposition among recent theologians that the unwary reader might be led to think there was nothing but disagreement and widening differences among contemporary religious thinkers. Such an impression would be radically mistaken.

## A TREND TO CONCILIATION

A prominent feature of American theology since 1950 has been a trend toward conciliation. A number of able writers are avowedly devoted to mediation between opposing schools of theological thought. Particularly is this true of Nils Ehrenstrom, John Coleman Bennett, and Walter Marshall Horton. Ehrenstrom is devoting his life to the ecumenical study of problems in theology and Christian ethics, and to work for unity of the churches. Bennett has for many years provided an especially useful bridge of communication between liberal and neo-Reformation centers of thought. Horton's increasing devotion to theological mediation on a world scale came to a climax in his volume, *Christian Theology: An Ecumenical Approach*.[1] Edward T. Ramsdell's *The Christian Perspective*[2] is explicitly directed to the conciliation of opposing views on the critical problem of theological method.

Most of Nels Ferré's writings are conciliatory in mood and substance. Paul Tillich's *Systematic Theology* draws much from opposing views and so furthers communication between them.

Albert Outler's excellent book *Psychotherapy and the Christian Message*[3] not only builds a strong new bridge between theology and psychotherapy but also states the Christian message in such irenic, inclusive terms as to provide a platform on which thinkers from varied points of departure can stand together.

Some tendencies toward mediation are appearing in unlikely places. Reinhold Niebuhr, despite his love of dramatic overstatement and his traditional severity with opposing views, appears increasingly in the role of mediator between American and German thought. The most intransigeant movement among Protestant theologians has been the fundamentalist. Yet even in that movement, as we have observed, such acknowledged and influential leaders as Harold Ockenga, Carl Henry and Edward John Carnell are making significant conciliatory gestures toward their more liberal contemporaries.

The ecumenical movement, especially through the World Council of Churches and its conferences on Faith and Order, has encouraged sustained, effective communication between opposing thinkers and helped to develop a special calling of theological concilation. Under official auspices of the World Council have been produced such mediating volumes as *The Nature of the Church*, edited by R. Newton Flew,[4] *The Realm of Redemption* by J. Robert Nelson,[5] and *Intercommunion*, edited by Donald M. Baillie and John Marsh.[6]

## OLD AGREEMENTS

In stressing the distinguishing characteristics of recent theology, we must not lose sight of deep agreements on certain broad historic doctrines and attitudes which are characteristic of Christianity generally. We must not make the mistake of one student who had heard a professor's criticism of a famous theologian, promptly labeled him as an enemy, and then was surprised to read one of his books and find he seemed to talk like a Christian! We must not mistake a discussion of differences within the family for a war with a foreign foe.

Though any given form of words is likely to stir misgivings or even provoke emphatic protests in some quarters within the church, it still remains true that an understanding Christian may go into almost any church, excepting possibly a few on the most extreme fringes of doctrine and practice, and experience there a familiar stirring of his conscience and his impulse to worship. The same Bible is read in Christian churches throughout the world, even though in many languages and different versions. Nearly everywhere there is the sacramental eating of consecrated bread and drinking of the consecrated cup with the repeating of familiar words attributed to Jesus in his last supper with his disciples before the crucifixion. In churches of every kind the cross appears as central, sacred symbol, whether in the medium of words, visual art, music, or in all these media. Everywhere there is the use of a prayer attributed to Jesus' instruction and beginning with the words which express the most daring, comforting, and revolutionary idea in Christian doctrine—"Our Father."

Generally present also is the conviction that God is the author of human life and its natural environment; that this life was intended to be and, when it reaches its rightful destiny, is good; that generous, self-giving love is the main principle of the good life; and that such life is to be lived in its fullness only by the help of God as revealed in the life of Jesus Christ, his willing sacrifice of himself on Calvary, and his resurrection. Wherever people call themselves Christians there is praise of loyal, monogamous marriage, self-disciplined purity of life, honesty, humility, prayer, efforts to live at peace with one's neighbors, and confident hope in life after death, with the expectation of ultimate triumph of righteousness over evil.

## NEW AGREEMENTS

These are no small agreements, and by comparison with them many theological differences look very small indeed. Yet even more encouraging for continued communication and collaboration among representatives of different theological movements are the *new* agreements in theology.

By "agreements" is not meant *unanimous* assent or exact identity of belief. Calling the agreements "new" does not mean that the ideas have never before been proposed or even widely believed. I do mean to say that *as compared with the recent past we have, in regard to these ideas, achieved a remarkable advance in the degree of agreement and in the variety of theologians subscribing to it*. Four items of such new agreement will here be proposed for consideration.

1. *Social Implications of the Gospel*. First of all, it is noteworthy that theologians of the widest diversity of tradition have been discovering that the Christian gospel has radical social implications. Outstanding Lutherans and Methodists, Anglicans and Friends, Eastern Orthodox and Baptists, lib-

erals, fundamentalists, and adherents of new Reformation theology are acknowledging that to take our faith seriously requires basic and far-reaching changes in our economic, political, and cultural institutions.

For decades just before and after 1900 the principal work in theology used by Methodist seminaries and ministers was *A Compendium of Christian Theology*, by William Burton Pope.[7] In this work he included his "Christian Ethics." Of the 110 pages devoted to this subject, he allotted less than three pages to "Ethics of Social and Commercial Relations" and less than two pages to "Political Ethics." Moreover, he saw nothing in Christian teaching critical of the prevailing methods of carrying on industry and commerce. The Bible nowhere contradicts it, he was sure; indeed, "in it all the laws of honest merchandise have the fullest sanction. In fact, every other theory is opposed by the tenour of Scripture." Regarding politics he was even more conservative, devoting most of his space to urging the Christian duties of "submission," "tribute," and "patriotism," while stressing that under any government the Christian is forbidden "personal insurrection and resistance."

Now contrast the easygoing social conformity of Pope with such a work as Reinhold Niebuhr's *Moral Man and Immoral Society*[8] or John C. Bennett's *Christian Ethics and Social Policy*[9] or Walter G. Muelder's *Foundations of the Responsible Society*[10] and you can see how far we have traveled since the beginning of this century.

It is not only in the American churches that the social radicalism of the gospel is being recognized. Traditionally, the Lutheran churches of the European continent have strictly refrained from criticizing the civil government, and this attitude has been defended by a long line of theologians from Luther to the present century. Yet the highly respected and influential Lutheran thinker, Bishop Gustaf Aulén, can now publish such a book as *Church, Law and Society*[11] and stir scarcely a ripple of theological protest. In this work he argues not only for the bold assumption of political responsibilities by individual Christians, but even insists that the church as church is obliged to speak out on specific economic and political issues.

Out of Eastern Orthodoxy has come that apostle of freedom, N. A. Berdyaev. He believed it impossible to separate the spiritual freedom of our Christian faith from the courageous battle for political and economic freedom. This battle must be waged against the tyranny and injustice of czarism, communism, and Western capitalism alike. He has made that crystal clear in his book *The Realm of Spirit and the Realm of Caesar*[12] and many other writings.

The most dramatic and doctrinally controversial theologian in the world today is undoubtedly Karl Barth. With all his stress on human sin and impotence, his doctrine that we live "between the times" of Christ's victory over sin at Calvary and the manifestation of that victory in his "coming again," and his neo-Calvinist emphasis on the sovereignty of God, Barth might not seem likely to be much concerned with social criticism or political action. Yet, not only does he write at length in many books and tracts for the justifying of such concern, including hundreds of pages in his *Kirchliche Dogmatik*,[13] but he has spoken out and acted so boldly and radically, though erratically, in political affairs, as to be hardly less controversial in politics than in theology.

As we have seen earlier, even among American fundamentalists, some who take the theological study of the Bible in dead earnest, and not merely as a means of finding texts by which to support preconceived prejudices, are seeing anew the important social message of the Scriptures. Significant of this discovery is a book already mentioned, *The Uneasy Conscience of Modern Fundamentalism*, by Carl F. H. Henry.[14]

Henry not only decries the "reluctance" of most fundamentalists "to come to grip with social evils," but warns against "unstudied and superficial analysis of the specific modern evils."

Especially impressive are the declarations on social problems contained in the Message of the Evanston Assembly to the churches. What is said there is no mere reflection of what is being said by the public generally! That representatives of such

varied churches, widely diverse theologies and geo-
graphically far-flung cultures could reach a substan-
tial degree of agreement on such a distinctive
utterance on a wide range of social problems is
highly significant.

It may be a long while before the practices of
church organizations and the opinions of the rank-
and-file membership in the churches are brought
to the level of the social conscience declared in the
Evanston report on race relations. Yet there has
rapidly developed among the leading Christian
theologians of many lands a remarkable measure of
new agreement on this issue. Evidences of similarly
converging views on a number of other social issues
are heartening.

2. *The Word Behind the Words.* A second area
of widening new agreement concerns the authority
of the Bible.

A significant advance of the past twenty-five years
has been the rediscovery of the soul-searching, expe-
rience-interpreting and life-creating truth to be
found by reverent study of the Scriptures. But this
does not mean that the critical advances made in
biblical studies in the preceding fifty years have
been lost. To be sure, every social trend has its
excesses. Some theologians who have rediscovered
the value of the Bible, have, in their enthusiasm,
fallen easily into the old uncritical, proof-texting
ways. But on the principal thinkers of Christendom
the liberal, critical studies of the Bible have left a

deep mark. There is a radical difference between the imaginative, creative way in which a Barth, a Brunner, or a Reinhold Niebuhr uses the Bible and the way Calvin, Luther, and Wesley felt obliged to use it, even though the great Reformers were far more candidly and critically selective than most of their contemporaries.

In the present new stress on biblical truth, there is emerging a remarkable breadth of agreement on this doctrine: the authority of the distinctive Christian revelation does not reside primarily in the book which we now hold in our hands—whatever its version or language. It does reside in certain supremely revelatory events which the biblical writings report to us.

To many writers, like H. H. Rowley, T. H. and T. W. Manson, Elmer A. Leslie, Bernhard Anderson, Amos N. Wilder, and a host of others, this doctrine implies that we should use every possible historical and literary skill to reconstruct the historical events, in order to understand in ancient context the original intent of the biblical authors and of the oral traditions which they interpreted and recorded. Most biblical scholars would grant the propriety of such reconstructions and understandings so far as they are possible. But many would doubt that concerning some of the most important matters they are possible to a very high degree. Even when they are possible, some scholars would emphasize the thought that other requirements are far more important if the essential message is to be received today. Thus Paul S. Minear stresses the reading with "eyes of faith,"[15] while Barth teaches the necessity that the "Word as written" be accompanied by the "Word as preached" and the "Word as revealed," so that the God who spoke long ago may speak anew, across the centuries, to the present worshiper, despite the infinite distance which separates us from Him.[16]

Such views may lead, as in the work of men like Minear, Rudolf Bultmann, Clarence Craig, Robert H. Pfeiffer, and John Knox, to the most searching historical criticism, without diminishing a profound personal reverence in the presence of what is regarded as divine revelation *through* the Scriptures. These men are about as far removed as possible from the slavish literalism which was often evident in the precritical centuries. Yet they have had important roles in the great resurgence of belief in the authority of the biblical revelation. Karl Barth, though apparently attaching little importance to historical criticism and sometimes using passages out of context in rather reckless fashion, still exemplifies a discriminating freedom in his study of the Scriptures which would hardly be possible if he held to a doctrine of the literal divine authority of the printed page in his hands.

Even the recent changes observed among some of the better conservative scholars point in this direction.

When Edward John Carnell welcomes and praises textual criticism for taking us nearer to the infallible *autographa* he is, to be sure, taking a view which is not likely to remain stable very long. The rigorous distinction he makes between the textual criticism which he blesses and the historical criticism which he sharply condemns, will prove impossible to maintain in practice. Many advances in textual criticism have been dependent upon advances in historical criticism. Moreover, the theory of infallible *autographa* raises the question what can be meant by the "original" manuscripts of Genesis and other conspicuously composite books.

Nevertheless, these and other patent defects should not cause us to underestimate the importance of a development which leads some of the ablest conservative teachers to remove their supreme commitment from the printed page in hand and begin, at least in small measure, the process of critical discrimination in the study of the Bible. One good result is that it opens the way for better communication between them and more liberal leaders, a process devoutly to be desired for the mutual strengthening of us all in a wider Christian fellowship.

3. *Decisive Commitment.* A third new agreement concerns the necessity of absolute commitment.

A tragedy of university life in the last generation was the mood of sophisticated indecision. Encouraged by the analogy of scientific doubt, the predominant attitude on questions of ultimate life purpose and of public policy alike was one of open-minded and easygoing tolerance. Fanaticism was regarded as the one real sin, and many professors were noted for their artful fence-straddling on matters of supreme importance. At the same time, encouraged by the analogy of biological evolution, there came into great vogue the doctrine that all true progress, whether of individual or society, was accomplished gradually, by minute increments of advance. This gradualism encouraged the easygoing tendency to avoid decisive commitments, to be content with slight inclinations in the direction of truth and right, and at all times to keep open convenient ways of retreat.

This tendency moved from the universities out into the whole fabric of society and deeply permeated the life of the churches. In the more liberal circles its effect was most clearly seen in the neglect of calls to personal repentance and avoidance of such embarrassing doctrines as Jesus' teaching about the new birth. In the conservative churches it affected most the attitudes toward social issues, such churches generally accepting social institutions as they were, or at most seeking some gradual amelioration in minor aspects, here or there.

Most theologians wrote little to challenge directly the prevailing mood, although some were not much affected by it. Then came the crisis theology of Karl Barth and Emil Brunner, with a great surge of interest in the existentialism of Sören Kierkegaard.

Both the crisis theologians and the Christian existentialists differ greatly within these schools of thought, as well as the two groups with each other. But they are alike in this, that they stress heavily the demand for absolute commitment. The Christian as they describe him is not a man who in some minor details of life is a little different from the non-Christian, while he is in process of further growth. Nor is he one who is characterized chiefly by thinking that on the whole certain propositions seem more probably true than others. Rather, he has ventured the decisive step. He has taken sides. He has chosen Christ and entered into a solemn covenant with God which makes everything different for him, from the inside out, from his private meditations to the farthest reaches of his social relations, from now to eternity.

This doctrine has been expounded with many excesses and aberrations which are doomed. But the stress on decisive commitment is gaining ground continually. In this country, for example, it is emphasized not only by men like Reinhold Niebuhr and H. Richard Niebuhr, but also by such radically different theologians as Henry Pitney Van Dusen, Edwin Lewis, Walter M. Horton, Nels Ferré, and Walter G. Muelder.

History favors this insight. Recent world events must have impressed every thoughtful person with the momentous necessity of decision. In some things neutrality and tentativeness are impossible. Again and again it has been demonstrated that for individuals, churches, and nations alike there are sometimes moments when not to decide is nevertheless to decide for life or death. As a matter of fact, the universality of death itself makes it inevitable that not only part but all of every life will be given up to something. The absoluteness of this giving we cannot gainsay. We can only say to *what* we are given and whether we make the commitment with the understanding of its absolute character and in a spirit appropriate to such absoluteness.

It is not necessary to take the view of some existentialists that we must decide the ultimate issues of life by reckless gambles of the will without rational guidance. Such a view seems neither true nor wise. Yet, on the other hand, no amount of study, search, and argument in quest of light on the ultimate issues will be of any practical good if we do not commit ourselves honestly, decisively, and boldly to live by the truth we find. If we wait until all the evidence is in before making commitment, we shall be always waiting, meanwhile giving our lives to ends in which we do not truly believe. Not to decide is yet to decide, but to decide halfheartedly, ambiguously, and often far below the level of the best evidence in hand. The need is for people who will decide thoughtfully and deliberately for discipleship to Jesus Christ and then raise a banner to which others can rally.

4. *Rediscovery of the Church.* The fourth area of new agreement is in the rediscovery of the church.

Protestant Christians, from the Reformation to the present time, have found offensive the papal claim, "Outside the church there is no salvation." In Roman Catholic usage this means that salvation is mediated exclusively by the ecclesiastical organization under the rule of the pope. In rebuking this claim, Protestants have been inclined to describe the redemptive relationship as a purely individual affair, involving a man and God. This tendency, particularly in America, was encouraged by the stress on individualism in our secular economic, political, and cultural life, until it went far beyond anything envisaged by Luther or Calvin. Indeed, so extreme had become this individualistic interpretation of our faith that many ministers found it hard to answer the claim of some men that they could be "just as good Christians alone as in the church." In some denominations very little attention was paid to doctrines concerning the church.

Contrast, then, the new stress on the church in recent Protestant thought. Of course, the Anglo-Catholics would be expected to emphasize it. Undoubtedly the prominence of Anglicans in the ecumenical movement has fostered it. But under all kinds of independent auspices a similar interest has arisen. Indeed, some of the religious experiments which have most affected recent discussions of the church have been at the opposite end of the spec-

trum from the Anglicans, that is, among the
Quakers.

Of course Anglicans and Quakers have far different conceptions of the redemptive society. But the
Friend, Elton Trueblood, no less than did the late
Archbishop William Temple, believes in the indis-
pensability of the Christian fellowship. Meanwhile,
the British Methodist R. Newton Flew has written
extensively on the doctrine of the church and edited
an ecumenical symposium on the subject for the
World Council of Churches.[17] Another Methodist,
J. Robert Nelson, has published a fine historical
and critical study under the title, *The Realm of
Redemption*.[18] Nels Ferré's earlier book, *Christian
Fellowship*,[19] was representative of the best thinking
in the churches of congregational polity.

As signs of the present new agreement in empha-
sizing the indispensable significance of the church,
even the books on doctrine of the church are less
decisive than the central place which the church
occupies in most recent general works in systematic
theology. The very titles reveal this emphasis. For
example, Karl Barth's multivolume work is not
merely *Dogmatik*, but *Die Kirchliche Dogmatik*;
Gustaf Aulén's concise interpretation of Lutheran
theology is not "The Christian Faith," but *The
Faith of the Christian Church*. Similarly, both the
method and the conclusion of my own systematic
theology required that it be called *A Theology of
the Living Church*. Even where the title does not

indicate it, however, the church is likely to be found in a highly significant place.

This new emphasis on the doctrine of the church is acknowledgment of the profoundly social nature of human persons. No Christian has learned his faith by himself. The historical stream of Christian fellowship, study, and testimony has brought to us the living, transforming Word of God. Without the ministry of others none of us could ever have learned of Christ. Moreover, we could not now live Christian lives in voluntary isolation from one another. For to love God is to love also our neighbors and to be drawn into the *koinonia*, the fellowship of sharing with other faithful men. In relation to this fact, the clashing conceptions of organizational forms seem more significant as barriers to the unity for which Christ prayed than for the special values of which each is regarded as guardian. There is an increasingly urgent conviction among Christians that they belong together and that men ought not to put asunder those whom God's purpose has drawn to a common supreme loyalty.

## NOTES

1. See above, Chap. 2, n. 4.
2. New York: Abingdon-Cokesbury Press, 1950.
3. New York: Harper & Brothers, 1954.
4. London: SCM Press, 1952.
5. London: Epworth Press, 1951.

6. London: SCM Press, 1952.
7. Second edition (New York: Phillips and Hunt, 1880).
8. New York: Charles Scribner's Sons, 1932.
9. New York: Charles Scribner's Sons, 1946.
10. Nashville, Tenn.: Abingdon Press, 1959.
11. New York: Charles Scribner's Sons, 1948.
12. London: Gollancz, 1952.
13. Zürich: Evangelischer Verlag, 1947.
14. See above, Chap. 3, n. 1.
15. See his book *Eyes of Faith* (Philadelphia: The Westminster Press, 1946).
16. *The Doctrine of the Word of God* (New York: Charles Scribner's Sons, 1936), pp. 98-212.
17. See above, Chap. 6, n. 4.
18. See above, Chap. 6, n. 5.
19. New York: Harper & Brothers, c. 1940.

# CHAPTER SEVEN

# UNSETTLED ISSUES

There are many important theological questions concerning which disagreement continues. Some of them divide church from church. Others cut across denominational lines.

## SOME DIFFERENCES AMONG THE CHURCHES

In many matters the Roman Catholic church stands altogether alone. Members of that church differ from all others in maintaining the doctrinal infallibility of the pope when he speaks as pope, in solemn proclamation to all the faithful. In general, only Roman Catholics hold the doctrine of transubstantiation, that is, the teaching that in the Mass, literally, the very substance of the body of Christ is present and there is then no substance of bread or wine remaining. The Eastern Orthodox doctrine is similar, but leaves room for more of mystery and of spiritual interpretation. The Lutheran churches teach that the true body of Christ is present in the Eucharist, to those who receive it in faith, but do not deny that the bread and wine are also present. Most other Protestants stress the spiritual presence of Christ or regard the sacrament as purely symbolic.

Roman Catholics are alone in the amount of attention given to the Virgin Mary and the near-deification of her person. Their church, alone, accepts the doctrine of the Immaculate Conception (that is, miraculous conception without Original Sin), of Mary in her mother's womb and the Assumption, that is, the miraculous conveying of the body of Mary into Heaven. Though some Anglicans and also the Eastern Orthodox believe in an intermediate state, or Purgatory, in which the redeemed are purified for life in Heaven, the Roman Catholics alone maintain an elaborate system of doctrine about Purgatory and believe in merits and indulgences by which their time in Purgatory can be shortened by the words or actions of their survivors on earth.

The Roman Catholics, the Eastern Orthodox, and some Anglo-Catholics believe in seven sacraments, as follows: baptism, confirmation, penance, Eucharist (or Mass), matrimony, Extreme Unction (or Unction of the Sick), and ordination. Most Protestants regard only baptism and the Eucharist (Lord's Supper or Holy Communion) as sacraments. They would generally regard confirmation (or reception of members into the church), matrimony, and ordination as solemn and sacred rites, but they do not count them as sacraments, either because they were not established by Jesus Christ or because they are not open to all in the church. In most Protestant churches there are no formal rites of penance—though many calls to *repentance!*—nor of extreme unction. The Society of Friends recognizes no formal sacraments, though the Friends acknowledge the sacramental character of many acts in our common life.

The interpretations of the authority and office of the clergy varies greatly, from those Friends' organizations ("Meetings") which have no clergy at all, and Jehovah's Witnesses, who regard all their people as ministers, to the Roman Catholic church, which acknowledges the priesthood only of men who are under the authority of the pope and who were ordained by bishops who are believed to be in a continuous line formed by the laying on of hands by bishops, reaching back to Simon Peter and Jesus. Eastern Orthodox churchmen and many Anglicans also believe that a valid priesthood or ministry requires the unbroken "Apostolic Succession," but of course they do not accept subjection to the pope. Most other Protestant churches have ordained ministers, but their authority with their people usually rests upon the belief that they are duly recognized by the church as living and preaching in the "true apostolic succession" of the teachings and spirit of Christ, with the blessing of the

Holy Spirit, and have been given such specialized education for the ministry as to equip them with superior knowledge in matters of faith and Christian practice.

There is newly widened agreement on the importance of the Church as the fellowship of believers under the Lordship of Christ and in the power of the Holy Spirit, but there continues to be wide disagreement about the relation between this true fellowship of believers and the organized churches. The Roman Catholic church teaches that it alone is the church; other churches are only falsely so-called. It therefore declines all the invitations to participate in the World Council of Churches. The Eastern Orthodox churches maintain that only in communion with the true ancient apostolic church are human beings saved, and formally they regard Eastern Orthodoxy as constituting the true church. However, some of them actively participate, with certain reservations, in the studies and other work of the World Council of Churches, in which most Protestant churches are represented, and their relations with the Church of England are especially cordial.

Some churches regard all the baptized persons of their countries as their members; others make strict demands of conduct and study under instruction. Some require convincing evidence of a personal experience of being "born again" before reception into membership or even baptism, which

is then known—for example, among the Baptists—
as "believers' baptism."

Most Protestants acknowledge that there are other
genuine Christian churches besides their own particular denominations. Some, like the Methodist
church and many Congregational churches, freely
receive members from various other churches with
scarcely more ceremony than is employed in trans-
ferring members from one local congregation to
another of the same denomination. Indeed, among
a number of the largest Protestant denominations,
even ministers are transferred with relatively little
difficulty. In defining what constitutes a true church,
some, like the Lutheran and Presbyterian churches,
would especially stress acceptable doctrine, but
would also specify proper administration of the
sacraments and Christian conduct. Others, like the
Methodist and various smaller bodies, though not
taking doctrine and sacraments lightly, would
chiefly emphasize inner loyalty and obedience to
Christ and conduct fittingly expressing such fidelity.

## OTHER THEOLOGICAL DIFFERENCES

Many questions of faith divide present Christian
thought along lines which cut across denominational
boundaries. Through the sometimes technical language of the theologians may be discovered issues
of wide variety.

1. The relations of revelation, reason, and faith
continue to get much attention. Are there some

things we know by reason and others by revelation? Or should we say that reason uses evidence from all sources, including revelation? Are there any sources of truth which do not involve revelation? Can a scientist learn anything in his laboratory if God does not act? Should God's regular activity in nature be regarded as revelation, or should that term be restricted to distinctive acts of God at particular times and places? May we find use here for the traditional distinction between general revelation and special revelation? If so, along what lines should we distinguish them? Is general revelation the regular self-disclosing activity of God in the orderly changes of nature, while special revelation is his self-disclosure to a particular person or group, in a particular time and place? Or would such a view imply a closer relation than exists between God and the world? Should we adopt Calvin's distinction between God's indirect word through his creation and his direct word given when he "opens his own sacred mouth"[1]? If so, what, precisely, is meant by the quoted figure of speech?

How is faith related to knowledge? Can we distinguish sharply between knowledge and faith, or is faith actually involved in all knowledge? Does faith make absolute, in practice, what reason finds probable in theory? Or is faith a different way of apprehending truth? What is the relation between intellectual belief and Christian faith? How is faith confirmed or validated?[2]

2. What is the place of the Bible in our religious knowledge? Is it merely the writings of some men, among the many who have sought to probe the mysteries of life and death and unseen power? Is it the infallible, miraculously given work of God himself, using inspired men as his instruments? Is it the fallible human record of God's "mighty acts" in human history? Precisely what is the relation between the words on the pages and the word of God himself?

3. What kind of being is God? Is he a person, that is a subject who thinks, loves, and wills—whatever else may be true of him? Is he a society of three individuals, more intimately related than any human individuals, but nevertheless sufficiently distinct so that they constitute a divine society? Or are the "three" spoken of in the doctrine of the Trinity three modes of revelation by the one individual Subject who is God? If three modes of revelation, do these modes represent also distinctions in the very being of God? Or is the doctrine of the Trinity a misconceived effort of the churches to express the transcendent, unchangeable majesty of God and at the same time his deep involvement in human affairs—as contended by Cyril C. Richardson?[3] How much can we know about Him? Do we know Him as he is, or only his action in relation to us? Should we worship Him primarily as inexpressible mystery, or rather as one whose wisdom,

power, and goodness are known to be worthy of
our highest reverence?

4. Who is Jesus? A religious genius who dis-
cerned many useful ideas by which to live ethically?
A divinely inspired prophet? A man whom God
chose to be the instrument of his supreme revelation of himself? God himself masquerading as a
man? God actually become man, while still continuing to be God, hence to our reason an utter
self-contradiction? Did the Jesus who talked with
his disciples in Galilee and prayed fervently to God
in Gethsemane live in heaven before he was born
in Palestine? If so, then while he was obeying
Joseph and Mary as a dutiful, young son in Naza-
reth, did he remember his heavenly experience before his birth? In what sense was the "Word"
which was "made flesh" in Jesus already existent
"in the beginning" and how did that Word participate in creation?[4] Was Jesus God, or the Son of
God? In precisely what sense?

5. What is the true nature of man? Is he only a
curious, freakish offspring of biological accident?
Why does he have this strange feeling of guilt about
himself? Why can he not simply be what he is, like
a star or a frog? Why this haunting desire to
achieve and to be more than now? Is man "little
less than God," as declared in Psalm 8, or is he a
miserable sinner, utterly worthless in himself but
treated as of great value by the free grace of God?
Is he best understood as created morally neutral

but potentially either good or bad? Or as made in the image of God, but fallen into sin and so estranged from his Maker and his own rightful destiny? Is the "image of God" in man a similarity between the very natures of man and God, or is it a relation to God in which God may be reflected in him, as the image of a human face is reflected in a mirror? Who is God? Who is Jesus? Who am I? These three questions are deeply interpenetrating. All three must be asked anew and answered for ourselves in every generation of the church.

6. Toward what end are we moving? In the continual ebb and flow of good and evil in the world, what will have the last word? Christian faith always affirms that God will win the victory in the end. But how does his Kingdom come? Does He alone bring it, in his own good time? Or does the time depend in part upon our obedient choice to do his will? Will the Kingdom ever "come on earth as it is in heaven"? Will all the confusions, fears, and strivings of our present earthly life be ended by the perfect reign of God, one day in history? Will his reign be established in glory after the earthly history of man has ended? Is it already present, but in the heavenly life of the faithful who have departed from this earth? Will the ultimate triumph of God be a victory of his love in every individual life? Or will the last word of God to some persons be the word of condemnation? Will the free choice of every human will finally be won to God by the

resourceful efforts of his love? Or will the last choices, like the present choices, of men, remain uncertain and often disastrous?

7. What does God require of us here and now? What is his will for our conduct in this present life? Christians agree that love is "the first and great commandment."[5] But precisely what is love, and what does love require in the complex social problems of the twentieth century? Must we choose love in personal relations, but turn from love to a loveless justice in international affairs? How can we love our most ruthless enemies without betraying our most dependent friends? On the other hand, how can we protect even our friends when the weapons to be chosen in any serious war are of such abysmal destructiveness as to threaten all human life? What risks should love take?

In regard to race relations, very nearly all serious Christian theologians today are agreed that segregation and discrimination violate the will of God. This great measure of agreement has been but recently achieved, and is encouraging. But how far are the coercions of law to be used in the service of interracial justice and integration? How shall the Christian ideal of interracial brotherhood be realized in the face of determined opposition?

What is the way of love in courts of penal justice? Or is this a false question to ask? Is justice simply an impersonal order between the lines of which love must find such expression as it can? Can love reformulate justice so that justice becomes the appropriate expression of love in complex situations?

These and many other urgent problems of Christian ethics perplex and frequently divide even the best religious thinkers of our day.

## Questions and the Answer

Is it not discouraging that so many questions are still subjects of differing opinions among men and even among people who profess the same Lord?

Yes, to the earnest inquirer, eager and impatient for truth, it is discouraging. Yet it is encouraging, too, that so many fine minds and spirits are so urgently asking such questions today.

Where there is no inquiry there is no solution. Where people ask only how to gain more power—of wealth, of political rule, or of nuclear missiles— they do not learn how to use the power in the service of life, though they may learn how to destroy all life.

If our decisions are to be guided and our lives undergirded by the steadfastness of faith and by the wisdom and power of God, then faith must be virile and contemporary. Faith can be so, despite peril and persecution. But faith cannot flourish where only questions of technique are asked with earnestness and where men think of God only conventionally, superficially, and trivially.

It is encouraging that many wise and finely disciplined minds are today giving deep-searching, heartening answers to the ultimate questions of our existence. It is even more encouraging that so great a company of people, in all walks of life, are with real earnestness asking the ultimate questions. Where such questions are asked, there, even above the clamor of dissident voices, the answer of God himself may be heard. Where God himself is heard and obeyed, there are love, joy, and peace, even while the quest for more understanding continues.

## NOTES

1. *Institutes of the Christian Religion* (Philadelphia: Presbyterian Board of Christian Education, 1936), Book I, Chap. 6, 1.
2. In this book the author does not attempt to set forth his own views. However, he would not wish the reader to think him an evader of such issues as are raised here. Most of the questions raised in this chapter are confronted and the attempt made to find the answers, in the following four of his books: *The Religious Revolt Against Reason* (New York: Harper & Brothers, 1949); *A Theology of the Living Church* (New York: Harper & Brothers, 1953); *The Case for Theology in Liberal Perspective* (Philadelphia: The Westminster Press, 1959); *The Enduring Message of the Bible* (New York: Harper & Brothers, 1960). In them will be found also references to many books by other authors arriving at different conclusions.
3. See his book, *The Doctrine of the Trinity* (Nashville, Tenn.: Abingdon Press, 1958).
4. Cf. John 1:1-3, 14.
5. Matthew 22:38 (KJV).

# INDEX OF NAMES

## INDEX OF NAMES

Liberalism – Rauschenbusch
Gladden, Fosdick, u.s.w.


Fundamentalism – Evangelism
Machen – Buswell – Graham
☉ Fundamentals


Existentialism –
Kierkegaard

Bultmann
Tillich

Neo – Reformation
Barth
Brunner
Niebuhr